ECONOMIC SCIENCE
AND THE
AUSTRIAN METHOD

ECONOMIC SCIENCE
AND THE
AUSTRIAN METHOD

HANS-HERMANN HOPPE

Ludwig
von Mises
Institute
AUBURN, ALABAMA

Copyright © 1995 and 2007 by the Ludwig von Mises Institute

Ludwig von Mises Institute, 518 West Magnolia Avenue, Auburn, Ala. 36832; www.mises.org

ISBN 10 digit: 1-933550-11-2
ISBN 13 digit: 978-1-933550-11-4

Contents

PREFACE

It was a tragic day when economics, the queen of the social sciences, adopted the methods associated with the natural sciences: empiricism and positivism. In the sweep of economic thought, this change occurred—not coincidentally—about the same time that intellectuals and politicians came to believe in the efficacy of government planning. Despite their failures, both doctrines remain godless faiths of our age.

In this extraordinary essay, Hans-Hermann Hoppe extends the argument of Ludwig von Mises that the methods associated with natural sciences cannot be successfully appropriated for economic theory. Professor Hoppe then argues for the existence of a priori knowledge, the validity of pure theory, the use of deductive logic, the implacability of economic law, and the view that economics is but a part of the larger discipline of praxeology: the science of human action.

If economists are to free themselves from the failed assumptions that they can precisely predict the future and, thus, that the state can plan the economy better than the market, they will have to revisit more fundamental methodological errors. When that happens, Professor Hoppe, the outstanding praxeologist working today, will have played an indispensable role.

—Llewellyn H. Rockwell, Jr.
Ludwig von Mises Institute

PRAXEOLOGY AND
ECONOMIC SCIENCE

I t is well-known that Austrians disagree strongly with other schools of economic thought, such as the Keynesians, the Monetarists, the Public Choicers, Historicists, Institutionalists, and Marxists.[1] Disagreement is most conspicuous, of course, when it comes to economic policy and economic policy proposals. At times there also exists an alliance between Austrians and, in particular, Chicagoites and Public Choicers. Ludwig von Mises, Murray N. Rothbard, Milton Friedman, and James Buchanan, to cite a few names, are often united in their efforts to defend the free market economy against its "liberal" and socialist detractors.

Nonetheless, as important as such occasional agreements may be for tactical or strategic reasons, they can only be superficial, for they cover up some truly fundamental differences between the Austrian school, as represented by Mises and Rothbard, and all the rest. The ultimate difference from which all disagreements at the levels of economic theory and economic policy stem—disagreements, for instance,

---

[1]The first two essays are based on two lectures delivered at the Ludwig von Mises Institute's "Advanced Instructional Conference on Austrian Economics," June 21–27, 1987. The third essay is reprinted from *The Economics and Ethics of Private Property* (Kluwer Academic Publishers in 1993), pp. 141–64.

as regards the merit of the gold standard vs. fiat money, free-banking vs. central banking, the welfare implications of markets vs. state-action, capitalism vs. socialism, the theory of interest and the business cycle, etc.—concerns the answer to the very first question that any economist must raise: What is the subject matter of economics, and what kind of propositions are economic theorems?

Mises's answer is that economics is the science of human action. In itself, this may not sound very controversial. But then Mises says of the science of economics:

> Its statements and propositions are not derived from experience. They are, like those of logic and mathematics, a priori. They are not subject to verification and falsification on the ground of experience and facts. They are both logically and temporally antecedent to any comprehension of historical facts. They are a necessary requirement of any intellectual grasp of historical events.[2]

In order to emphasize the status of economics as a pure science, a science that has more in common with a discipline like applied logic than, for instance, with the empirical natural sciences, Mises proposes the term "praxeology" (the logic of action) for the branch of knowledge exemplified by economics.[3]

It is this assessment of economics as an a priori science, a science whose propositions can be given a rigorous logical justification, which distinguishes Austrians, or more

---

[2]Ludwig von Mises, *Human Action* (Chicago: Henry Regnery, 1966), p. 32.

[3]Mises's methodological work is contained mainly in his *Epistemological Problems of Economics* (New York: New York University Press, 1981); *Theory and History* (Washington, D.C.: Ludwig von Mises Institute, 1985); *The Ultimate Foundation of Economic Science* (Kansas City, Kans.: Sheed Andrews and McMeel, 1978); *Human Action*, part I.

precisely Misesians, from all other current economic schools. All the others conceive of economics as an empirical science, as a science like physics, which develops hypotheses that require continual empirical testing. And they all regard as dogmatic and unscientific Mises's view that economic theorems—like the law of marginal utility, or the law of returns, or the time-preference theory of interest and the Austrian business cycle theory—can be given definite proof, such that it can be shown to be plainly contradictory to deny their validity.

The view of Mark Blaug, highly representative of mainstream methodological thought, illustrates this almost universal opposition to Austrianism. Blaug says of Mises, "His writings on the foundations of economic science are so cranky and idiosyncratic that one can only wonder that they have been taken seriously by anyone."[4]

Blaug does not provide one argument to substantiate his outrage. His chapter on Austrianism simply ends with that statement. Could it be that Blaug's and others' rejection of Mises's apriorism may have more to do with the fact that the demanding standards of argumentative rigor, which an apriorist methodology implies, prove too much for them?[5]

---

[4]Mark Blaug, *The Methodology of Economics* (Cambridge: Cambridge University Press, 1980), p. 93; for a similar statement of outrage see Paul Samuelson, *Collected Scientific Papers*, vol. 3 (Cambridge, Mass.: Harvard University Press, 1972), p. 761.

[5]Another prominent critic of praxeology is Terence W. Hutchison, *The Significance and Basic Postulates of Economic Theory* (London: Macmillan, 1938). Hutchison, like Blaug an adherent of the Popperian variant of empiricism, has since become much less enthusiastic about the prospects of advancing economics along empiricist lines (see, for instance, his *Knowledge and Ignorance in Economics* [Chicago: University of Chicago Press, 1977]; and *The Politics and Philosophy of Economics* [New York: New York University Press, 1981]), yet he still sees no alternative to Popper's falsificationism. A position and development quite similar

What led Mises to his characterization of economics as an a priori science? From the present day perspective it might be surprising to hear that Mises did not see his conception as out of line with the mainstream view prevailing in the early twentieth century. Mises did not wish to prescribe what economists should be doing as opposed to what they actually were doing. Rather, he saw his achievement as a philosopher of economics in systematizing, and in making explicit what economics really was, and how it had implicitly been conceived by almost everyone calling himself an economist.

And this is indeed the case. In giving a systematic explanation of what was formerly only implicit and unspoken knowledge, Mises did introduce some conceptual and terminological distinctions that had previously been unclear and unfamiliar, at least to the English-speaking world. But his position on the status of economics was essentially in full agreement with the then-orthodox view on the matter. They did not employ the term "a priori," but such mainstream economists as Jean Baptiste Say, Nassau Senior, and John E. Cairnes, for instance, described economics quite similarly.

Say writes: "A treatise on political economy will . . . be confined to the enunciation of a few general principles, not requiring even the support of proofs or illustrations; because

to Hutchison's is to be found in H. Albert (see his earlier *Marktsoziologie und Entscheidungslogik* (Neuwied: 1967). For a critique of the empiricist position, see Hans-Hermann Hoppe, *Kritik der kausalwissenschaftlichen Sozialforschung. Untersuchungen zur Grundlegung von Soziologie und Ökonomie* (Opladen: 1983); "Is Research Based on Causal Scientific Principles Possible in the Social Sciences?" *Ratio* 25, no. 1 (1983); "In Defense of Extreme Rationalism," *Review of Austrian Economics* 3 (1988); "On Praxeology and the Praxeological Foundations of Epistemology and Ethics," in Llewellyn H. Rockwell, Jr., ed., *The Meaning of Ludwig von Mises* (Auburn, Ala.: Ludwig von Mises Institute, 1989).

these will be but the expression of what every one will know, arranged in a form convenient for comprehending them, as well as in their whole scope as in their relation to each other." And "political economy . . . whenever the principles which constitute its basis are the rigorous deductions of undeniable general facts, rests upon an immovable foundation."[6]

According to Nassau Senior, economic "premises consist of a few general propositions, the result of observations, or consciousness, and scarcely requiring proof, or even formal statement, which almost every man, as soon as he hears them, admits as familiar to his thoughts, or at least as included in his previous knowledge; and his inferences are nearly as general, and, if he has reasoned correctly, as certain as his premises." And economists should be "aware that the Science depends more on reasoning than on observation, and that its principal difficulty consists not in the ascertainment of its facts, but in the use of its terms."[7]

And John E. Cairnes remarks that while "mankind has no direct knowledge of ultimate physical principles" . . . "the economist starts with a knowledge of ultimate causes." . . . "The economist may thus be considered at the outset of his researches as already in possession of those ultimate principles governing the phenomena which form the subject of his study, the discovery of which in the case of physical investigation constitutes for the inquirer his most arduous task." "Conjecture [in economics] would manifestly be out of place, inasmuch as we possess in our consciousness and

---

[6]Jean-Baptiste Say, *Treatise on Political Economy* (New York: Augustus Kelley, [1880] 1964), p. xx, xxvi.

[7]Nassau Senior, *An Outline of the Science of Political Economy* (New York: Augustus Kelley, [1836] 1965), pp. 2–3, 5.

in the testimony of our senses . . . direct and easy proof of that which we desire to know. In Political Economy, accordingly, hypothesis is never used as a help toward the discovery of ultimate causes and laws."[8]

The views of Mises's predecessors, Menger, Böhm-Bawerk, and Wieser, are the same: They, too, describe economics as a discipline whose propositions can—in contrast to those of the natural sciences—be given some ultimate justification. Again, however, they do so without using the terminology employed by Mises.[9]

And finally, Mises's epistemological characterization of economics was also considered quite orthodox—and certainly not idiosyncratic, as Blaug would have it—after having been explicitly formulated by Mises. Lionel Robbins's book *The Nature and Significance of Economic Science*, which first appeared in 1932, is nothing but a somewhat watered-down version of Mises's description of economics as praxeology. Yet it was respected by the economics profession as the guiding methodological star for almost twenty years.

In fact, Robbins, in his Preface, explicitly singles out Mises as the most important source of his own methodological position. And Mises and Richard von Strigl—whose

[8]John E. Cairnes, *The Character and Logical Method of Political Economy* (New York: Augustus Kelley, 1965), p. 83, 87, 89–90, 95–96.

[9]See Carl Menger, *Untersuchungen über die Methoden der Sozialwissenschaften* (Leipzig: 1883); idem, *Die Irrtümer des Historismus in der Deutschen Nationalökonomie* (Wien: 1884); Eugen von Böhm-Bawerk, *Schriften*, F. X. Weiss, ed. (Vienna: 1924); Friedrich von Wieser, *Theorie der gesellschaftlichen Wirtschaft* (Tübingen: 1914); idem, *Gesammelte Abhandlungen* (Tübingen: 1929). For Mises's evaluation of his predecessors, see his *Epistemological Problems of Economics*, pp. 17–22. The term "a priori" in connection with economic theorems is also used by Frank H. Knight; his methodological writings, however, lack systematic rigor. See his "What Is Truth in Economics," in Knight, *On the History and Method of Economics* (Chicago: University of Chicago Press, 1956); and his "The Limitations of Scientific Method in Economics," in Knight, *The Ethics of Competition* (Chicago: University of Chicago Press, 1935).

position is essentially indistinguishable from Mises's[10]—are cited approvingly in the text more often than anyone else.[11]

Yet, illuminating as all this may be for an assessment of the present-day situation, it is only history. What then is the rationale of the classical economists for regarding their science as different than the natural sciences? And what is behind Mises's explicit reconstruction of this difference as one between an a priori science and an aposteriori science? It was the recognition that the process of validation—the process of discovering whether some proposition is true or not—is different in one field of inquiry than in the other.

Let us first look briefly at the natural sciences. How do we know what the consequences will be if we subject some nature-given material to specified tests, let's say, if we mix it with another kind of material? Obviously we do not know before we actually try it and observe what happens. We can make a prediction, of course, but our prediction is only a hypothetical one, and observations are required to find out if we are right or wrong.

Moreover, even if we have observed some definite outcome, let's say that mixing the two materials leads to an explosion, can we then be sure that such an outcome will

---

[10]Richard von Strigl, *Die ökonomischen Kategorien und die Organisation der Wirtschaft* (Jena: 1923).

[11]It may be worth mentioning that Robbins's methodological position, much like Friedrich A. Hayek's, became increasingly less Misesian over time due mainly to the influence of Karl R. Popper, their colleague at the London School of Economics. See on this Lionel Robbins, *An Autobiography of an Economist* (London: Macmillan, 1976); Hayek's disagreement with Mises's idea of praxeology has been most recently restated in his "Einleitung" to Ludwig von Mises's *Erinnerungen* (Stuttgart: 1978). Mises's own, entirely negative verdict on Popper can be found in his *The Ultimate Foundation of Economic Science*, p. 70. In support of this verdict see also Hans H. Hoppe *Kritik der kausalwissenschaftlichen Sozialforschung* (Opladen: Westdeutscher Verlag, 1983), pp. 48–49.

invariably occur whenever we mix such materials? Again, the answer is no. Our predictions will still, and permanently, be hypothetical. It is possible that an explosion will only result if certain other conditions—*A*, *B*, and *C*—are fulfilled. We can only find out whether or not this is the case and what these other conditions are by engaging in a never-ending trial and error process. This enables us to improve our knowledge progressively about the range of application for our original hypothetical prediction.

Now let us turn to some typical economic propositions. Consider the validation process of a proposition such as the following: Whenever two people *A* and *B* engage in a voluntary exchange, they must both expect to profit from it. And they must have reverse preference orders for the goods and services exchanged so that *A* values what he receives from *B* more highly than what he gives to him, and *B* must evaluate the same things the other way around.

Or consider this: Whenever an exchange is not voluntary but coerced, one party profits at the expense of the other.

Or the law of marginal utility: Whenever the supply of a good increases by one additional unit, provided each unit is regarded as of equal serviceability by a person, the value attached to this unit must decrease. For this additional unit can only be employed as a means for the attainment of a goal that is considered less valuable than the least valued goal satisfied by a unit of such good if the supply were one unit shorter.

Or take the Ricardian law of association: Of two producers, if *A* is more productive in the production of two types of goods than is *B*, they can still engage in a mutually beneficial division of labor. This is because overall physical productivity is higher if *A* specializes in producing one good which he can produce most efficiently, rather than both *A* and *B* producing both goods separately and autonomously.

Or as another example: Whenever minimum wage laws are enforced that require wages to be higher than existing market wages, involuntary unemployment will result.

Or as a final example: Whenever the quantity of money is increased while the demand for money to be held as cash reserve on hand is unchanged, the purchasing power of money will fall.

Considering such propositions, is the validation process involved in establishing them as true or false of the same type as that involved in establishing a proposition in the natural sciences? Are these propositions hypothetical in the same sense as a proposition regarding the effects of mixing two types of natural materials? Do we have to test these economic propositions continuously against observations? And does it require a never-ending trial and error process in order to find out the range of application for these propositions and to gradually improve our knowledge, such as we have seen to be the case in the natural sciences?

It seems quite evident—except to most economists for the last forty years—that the answer to these questions is a clear and unambiguous No. That *A* and *B* must expect to profit and have reverse preference orders follows from our understanding of what an exchange is. And the same is the case concerning the consequences of a coerced exchange. It is inconceivable that things could ever be different: It was so a million years ago and it will be so a million years hence. And the range of application for these propositions too is clear once and for all: They are true whenever something is a voluntary exchange or a coerced exchange, and that is all there is to it.

There is no difference with respect to the other examples given. That the marginal utility of additional units of supply of homogeneous goods must fall follows from the incontestable statement that every acting person always prefers what satisfies him more over what satisfies him less. It is simply absurd to think that continuous testing would be required to establish such a proposition.

The Ricardian law of association, along with a once-and-for-all delineation of its range of application, also logically follows from the very existence of the situation described. If *A* and *B* differ as described and accordingly there exists a technological substitution ratio for the goods produced (one such rate for *A* and one for *B*), then if they engage in a division of labor as characterized by the law, the physical output produced must be greater than it otherwise would be. Any other conclusion is logically flawed.

The same is true regarding the consequences of minimum wage laws or an increase in the quantity of money. An increase in unemployment and a decrease in the purchasing power of money are consequences which are logically implied in the very description of the initial condition as stated in the propositions at hand. As a matter of fact, it is absurd to regard these predictions as hypothetical and to think that their validity could not be established independently of observations, i.e., other than by actually trying out minimum wage laws or printing more money and observing what happens.

To use an analogy, it is as if one wanted to establish the theorem of Pythagoras by actually measuring sides and angles of triangles. Just as anyone would have to comment on such an endeavor, mustn't we say that to think economic propositions would have to be empirically tested is a sign of outright intellectual confusion?

But Mises by no means merely notices this rather obvious difference between economics and the empirical sciences. He makes us understand the nature of this difference and explains how and why a unique discipline like economics, which teaches something about reality without requiring observations, can possibly exist. It is this achievement of Mises's which can hardly be overrated.

In order to better understand his explanation, we must make an excursion into the field of philosophy, or more precisely into the field of the philosophy of knowledge or epistemology. In particular, we must examine the epistemology of Immanuel Kant as developed most completely in his *Critique of Pure Reason*. Mises's idea of praxeology is clearly influenced by Kant. This is not to say that Mises is a plain and simple Kantian. As a matter of fact, as I will point out later, Mises carries the Kantian epistemology beyond the point at which Kant himself left off. Mises improves the Kantian philosophy in a way that to this very day has been completely ignored and unappreciated by orthodox Kantian philosophers. Nonetheless, Mises takes from Kant his central conceptual and terminological distinctions as well as some fundamental Kantian insights into the nature of human knowledge. Thus we must turn to Kant.

Kant, in the course of his critique of classical empiricism, in particular that of David Hume, developed the idea that all our propositions can be classified in a two-fold way: On the one hand they are either analytic or synthetic, and on the other they are either a priori or a posteriori. The meaning of these distinctions is, in short, the following. Propositions are analytic whenever the means of formal logic are sufficient in order to find out whether they are true or not; otherwise propositions are synthetic ones. And propositions are a posteriori whenever observations are necessary in order to establish their truth or at least confirm them. If observations are not necessary, then propositions are a priori.

The characteristic mark of Kantian philosophy is the claim that true a priori synthetic propositions exist—and it is because Mises subscribes to this claim that he can be called a Kantian. Synthetic a priori propositions are those whose truth-value can be definitely established, even though in order to do so the means of formal logic are not sufficient (while, of course, necessary) and observations are unnecessary.

According to Kant, mathematics and geometry provide examples of true a priori synthetic propositions. Yet he also thinks that a proposition such as the general principle of causality—i.e., the statement that there are time-invariantly operating causes, and every event is embedded into a network of such causes—is a true synthetic a priori proposition.

I cannot go into great detail here to explain how Kant justifies this view.[12] A few remarks will have to suffice. First, how is the truth of such propositions derived, if formal logic is not sufficient and observations are unnecessary? Kant's answer is that the truth follows from self-evident material axioms.

What makes these axioms self-evident? Kant answers, it is not because they are evident in a psychological sense, in which case we would be immediately aware of them. On the contrary, Kant insists, it is usually much more painstaking to discover such axioms than it is to discover some empirical truth such as that the leaves of trees are green. They are self-evident because one cannot deny their truth without self-contradiction; that is, in attempting to deny them one would actually, implicitly, admit their truth.

[12]A brilliant interpretation and justification of Kant's a prioristic epistemology is to be found in F. Kambartel, *Erfahrung und Struktur. Bausteine zu einer Kritik des Empirismus und Formalismus* (Frankfurt/M.: 1968), esp. chapter 3; see also Hans-Hermann Hoppe, *Handeln und Erkennen* (Bern: 1976).

How do we find such axioms? Kant answers, by reflecting upon ourselves, by understanding ourselves as knowing subjects. And this fact—that the truth of a priori synthetic propositions derives ultimately from inner, reflectively produced experience—also explains why such propositions can possibly have the status of being understood as necessarily true. Observational experience can only reveal things as they happen to be; there is nothing in it that indicates why things must be the way they are. Contrary to this, however, writes Kant, our reason can understand such things as being necessarily the way they are, "which it has itself produced according to its own design."[13]

In all this Mises follows Kant. Yet, as I said earlier, Mises adds one more extremely important insight that Kant had only vaguely glimpsed. It has been a common quarrel with Kantianism that this philosophy seemed to imply some sort of idealism. For if, as Kant sees it, true synthetic a priori propositions are propositions about how our mind works and must of necessity work, how can it be explained that such mental categories fit reality? How can it be explained, for instance, that reality conforms to the principle of causality if this principle has to be understood as one to which the operation of our mind must conform? Don't we have to make the absurd idealistic assumption that this is possible only because reality was actually created by the mind? So that I am not misunderstood, I do not think that such a charge against Kantianism is justified.[14] And yet,

[13]Immanuel Kant, *Kritik der reinen Vernunft*, in Kant, *Werke*, vol. 2, W. Weischedel, ed. (Wiesbaden: 1956), p. 23.

[14]See in particular F. Kambartel's work cited in note 12; instructive is also the Kant interpretation given by the biologist–ethologist K. Lorenz, *Vom Weltbild des Verhaltensforschers* (Munich: 1964); idem, *Die Rückseite des Spiegels. Versuch einer Naturgeschichte menschlichen Erkennens* (Munich: 1973). Among some followers

through parts of his formulations Kant has no doubt given this charge some plausibility.

Consider, for example, this programmatic statement of his: "So far it has been assumed that our knowledge had to conform to observational reality"; instead it should be assumed "that observational reality conform to our knowledge."[15]

Mises provides the solution to this challenge. It is true, as Kant says, that true synthetic a priori propositions are grounded in self-evident axioms and that these axioms have to be understood by reflection upon ourselves rather than being in any meaningful sense "observable." Yet we have to go one step further. We must recognize that such necessary truths are not simply categories of our mind, but that our mind is one of acting persons. Our mental categories have to be understood as ultimately grounded in categories of action. And as soon as this is recognized, all idealistic suggestions immediately disappear. Instead, an epistemology claiming the existence of true synthetic a priori propositions becomes a realistic epistemology. Since it is understood as ultimately grounded in categories of action, the gulf between the mental and the real, outside, physical world is bridged. As categories of action, they must be mental things as much as they are characteristics of reality. For it is through actions that the mind and reality make contact.

---

of Austrianism, the Kant interpretation of Ayn Rand (see, for instance, her *Introduction to Objectivist Epistemology* (New York: New American Library, 1979); or *For the New Intellectual* (New York: Random House, 1961) enjoys great popularity. Her interpretation, replete with sweeping denunciatory pronouncements, however, is characterized by a complete absence of any interpretive documentation whatsoever. See, on Rand's arrogant ignorance regarding Kant, B. Goldberg, "Ayn Rand's 'For the New Intellectual'," *New Individualist Review* 1, no. 3 (1961).

Kant had hinted at this solution. He thought mathematics, for instance, had to be grounded in our knowledge of the meaning of repetition, of repetitive operations. And he also realized, if only somewhat vaguely, that the principle of causality is implied in our understanding of what it is and means to act.[16]

Yet it is Mises who brings this insight to the foreground: Causality, he realizes, is a category of action. To act means to interfere at some earlier point in time in order to produce some later result, and thus every actor must presuppose the existence of constantly operating causes. Causality is a prerequisite of acting, as Mises puts it.

But Mises is not, as is Kant, interested in epistemology as such. With his recognition of action as the bridge between the mind and the outside reality, he has found a solution to the Kantian problem of how true synthetic a priori propositions can be possible. And he has offered some extremely valuable insights regarding the ultimate foundation of other central epistemological propositions besides the principle of causality, such as the law of contradiction as the cornerstone of logic. And he has thereby opened a path for future philosophical research that, to my knowledge, has hardly been traveled. Yet Mises's subject matter is economics, and so I will have to lay to rest the problem of explaining in more detail the causality principle as an a priori true proposition.[17]

---

[16]For Kantian interpretations of mathematics see H. Dingler, *Philosophie der Logik und Mathematik* (Munich: 1931); Paul Lorenzen, *Einführung in die operative Logik und Mathematik* (Frankfurt/M.: 1970); Ludwig Wittgenstein, *Remarks on the Foundations of Mathematics* (Cambridge, Mass.: M.I.T. Press, 1978); also Kambartel, *Erfahrung und Struktur*, pp. 118–22; for an unusually careful and cautious interpretation of Kantianism from the point of view of modern physics, see P. Mittelstaedt, *Philosophische Probleme der modernen Physik* (Mannheim: 1967).

[17]For some farther reaching considerations on these matters, see Hoppe "In Defense of Extreme Rationalism."

Mises not only recognizes that epistemology indirectly rests on our reflective knowledge of action and can thereby claim to state something a priori true about reality but that economics does so too and does so in a much more direct way. Economic propositions flow directly from our reflectively gained knowledge of action; and the status of these propositions as a priori true statements about something real is derived from our understanding of what Mises terms "the axiom of action."

This axiom, the proposition that humans act, fulfills the requirements precisely for a true synthetic a priori proposition. It cannot be denied that this proposition is true, since the denial would have to be categorized as an action—and so the truth of the statement literally cannot be undone. And the axiom is also not derived from observation—there are only bodily movements to be observed but no such things as actions—but stems instead from reflective understanding.

Moreover, as something that has to be understood rather than observed, it is still knowledge about reality. This is because the conceptual distinctions involved in this understanding are nothing less than the categories employed in the mind's interaction with the physical world by means of its own physical body. And the axiom of action in all its implications is certainly not self-evident in a psychological sense, although once made explicit it can be understood as an undeniably true proposition about something real and existent.[18]

Certainly, it is not psychologically evident nor is it observable that with every action an actor pursues a goal; and that whatever the goal may be, the fact that it is pursued

---

[18]On this and the following see Mises, *Human Action,* chapters IV,V.

by an actor reveals that he places a relatively higher value on it than on any other goal of action he could conceive of at the start of his action.

It is neither evident nor observable that in order to achieve his most highly valued goal an action must interfere or decide not to interfere (which, of course, is also an interference) at an earlier point in time to produce some later result; nor that such interferences invariably imply the employment of some scarce means (at least those of the actor's body, its standing room and the time absorbed by the interference).

It is neither self-evident nor can it be observed that these means must also have value for an actor—a value derived from that of the goal—because the actor must regard their employment as necessary in order to effectively achieve the goal; and that actions can only be performed sequentially, always involving the making of a choice, i.e., taking up that one course of action which at some given point in time promises the most highly valued result to the actor and excluding at the same time the pursuit of other, less highly valued goals.

It is not automatically clear or observable that as a consequence of having to choose and give preference to one goal over another—of not being able to realize all goals simultaneously—each and every action implies the incurrence of costs. For example, forsaking the value attached to the most highly valued alternative goal that cannot be realized or whose realization must be deferred because the means necessary to effect it are bound up in the production of another, even more highly valued goal.

And lastly, it is not plainly evident or observable that at its starting point every goal of action must be considered worth more to the actor than its cost and capable of yielding a profit, i.e., a result whose value is ranked higher than that of the foregone opportunities. And yet, every action is also invariably threatened by the possibility of a loss if an actor finds, in retrospect, that the result actually achieved—contrary to previous expectations—has a lower value than the relinquished alternative would have had.

All of these categories—values, ends, means, choice, preference, cost, profit and loss, as well as time and causality—are implied in the axiom of action. Yet, that one is able to interpret observations in such categories requires that one already knows what it means to act. No one who is not an actor could ever understand them. They are not "given," ready to be observed, but observational experience is cast in these terms as it is construed by an actor. Nor is their reflective reconstruction a simple, psychologically self-evident intellectual task, as proved by a long line of abortive attempts along the way to the just-outlined insights into the nature of action.

It took painstaking intellectual effort to recognize explicitly what, once made explicit, everybody recognizes immediately as true and can understand as true synthetic a priori statements, i.e., propositions that can be validated independently of observations and thus cannot possibly be falsified by any observation whatsoever.

The attempt to disprove the action-axiom would itself be an action aimed at a goal, requiring means, excluding other courses of action, incurring costs, subjecting the actor to the possibility of achieving or not achieving the desired goal and so leading to a profit or a loss.

And the very possession of such knowledge then can never be disputed, and the validity of these concepts can never be falsified by any contingent experience, for disputing or falsifying anything would already have presupposed their very existence. As a matter of fact, a situation in which these categories of action would cease to have a real existence could itself never be observed, for making an observation, too, is an action.

Mises's great insight was that economic reasoning has its foundation in just this understanding of action; and that the status of economics as a sort of applied logic derives from the status of the action-axiom as an a priori-true synthetic proposition. The laws of exchange, the law of diminishing marginal utility, the Ricardian law of association, the law of price controls, and the quantity theory of money—all the examples of economic propositions which I have mentioned—can be logically derived from this axiom. And this is why it strikes one as ridiculous to think of such propositions as being of the same epistemological type as those of the natural sciences. To think that they are, and accordingly to require testing for their validation, is like supposing that we had to engage in some fact-finding process without knowing the possible outcome in order to establish the fact that one is indeed an actor. In a word: It is absurd.

Praxeology says that all economic propositions which claim to be true must be shown to be deducible by means of formal logic from the incontestably true material knowledge regarding the meaning of action.

Specifically, all economic reasoning consists of the following:

(1) an understanding of the categories of action and the meaning of a change occurring in such things as values, preferences, knowledge, means, costs, etc;

(2) a description of a world in which the categories of action assume concrete meaning, where definite people are identified as actors with definite objects specified as their means of action, with some definite goals identified as values and definite things specified as costs. Such description could be one of a Robinson Crusoe world, or a world with more than one actor in which interpersonal relationships are possible; of a world of barter exchange or of money and exchanges that make use of money as a common medium of exchange; of a world of only land, labor, and time as factors of production, or a world with capital products; of a world with perfectly divisible or indivisible, specific or unspecific factors of production; or of a world with diverse social institutions, treating diverse actions as aggression and threatening them with physical punishment, etc; and

(3) a logical deduction of the consequences which result from the performance of some specified action within this world, or of the consequences which result for a specific actor if this situation is changed in a specified way.

Provided there is no flaw in the process of deduction, the conclusions that such reasoning yield must be valid a priori because their validity would ultimately go back to nothing but the indisputable axiom of action. If the situation and the changes introduced into it are fictional or assumptional (a Robinson Crusoe world, or a world with only indivisible or only completely specific factors of production), then the conclusions are, of course, a priori true only of such a "possible world." If, on the other hand, the situation and changes can be identified as real, perceived and conceptualized as such by real actors, then the conclusions are a priori true propositions about the world as it really is.[19]

---

[19]See also Hoppe, *Kritik der kausalwissenschaftlichen Sozialforschung*, chapter 3.

Such is the idea of economics as praxeology. And such then is the ultimate disagreement that Austrians have with their colleagues: Their pronouncements cannot be deduced from the axiom of action or even stand in clear-cut contradiction to propositions that can be deduced from the axiom of action.

And even if there is agreement on the identification of facts and the assessment of certain events as being related to each other as causes and consequences, this agreement is superficial. For such economists falsely believe their statements to be empirically well-tested propositions when they are, in fact, propositions that are true a priori.

II

Non-praxeological schools of thought mistakenly believe that relationships between certain events are well-established empirical laws when they are really necessary and logical praxeological ones. And they thereby behave as if the statement "a ball cannot be red and non-red all over at the same time" requires testing in Europe, America, Africa, Asia and Australia (of course requiring a lot of funds in order to pay for such daring nonsensical research). Moreover, the non-praxeologists also believe that relationships between certain events are well-established empirical laws (with predictive implications) when a priori reasoning can show them to be no more than information regarding contingent historical connections between events, which does not provide us with any knowledge whatsoever regarding the future course of events.

This illustrates another fundamental confusion non-Austrian schools have: a confusion over the categorical difference between theory and history and the implication that this difference has for the problem of social and economic forecasting.

I must again begin with a description of empiricism, the philosophy which thinks of economics and the social sciences in general as following the same logic of research as that, for instance, of physics. I will explain why. According to empiricism—today's most widely held view of economics—there is no categorical difference between theoretical and historical research. And I will explain what this implies for the idea of social forecasting. The very different Austrian view will then be developed out of a critique and refutation of the empiricist position.

Empiricism is characterized by the fact that it accepts two intimately related basic propositions.[20] The first and most central one is: Knowledge regarding reality, which is called empirical knowledge, must be verifiable or at least falsifiable by observational experience. Observational experience can only lead to contingent knowledge (as opposed to necessary knowledge), because it is always of such a kind that, in principle, it could have been different than it actually was. This means that no one can know in advance of experience—that

---

[20]For various representative accounts of empiricism—united in their opposition against any form of apriorism—see R. Carnap, *Der logische Aufbau der Welt* (Hamburg: 1966); idem, *Testability and Meaning* (New Haven, Conn.: Yale University Press, 1950); Alfred J. Ayer, *Logic, Truth, and Language* (New York: Dover, 1952); Karl R. Popper, *Logic of Scientific Discovery* (New York: Harper and Row, 1959); idem, *Conjectures and Refutations* (London: Routledge and Kegan Paul, 1969); C. G. Hempel, *Aspects of Scientific Explanation* (New York: Free Press, 1970); for accounts which also give some attention to economics, see in particular Ernest Nagel, *The Structure of Science* (New York: Harcourt, Brace and World, 1961); Felix Kaufmann, *Methodology of the Social Sciences* (Atlantic Highlands, N.J.: Humanities Press, 1944).

---

is before actually having had some particular observational experience—if the consequence of some real event will be one way or another. If, on the other hand, knowledge is not verifiable or falsifiable by observational experience, then it is not knowledge about anything real. It is simply knowledge about words, about the use of terms, about signs and transformational rules for signs. That is to say, it is analytical knowledge, but not empirical knowledge. And it is highly doubtful, according to this view, that analytical knowledge should be regarded as knowledge at all.

The second assumption of empiricism formulates the extension and application of the first assumption to problems of causality, causal explanation, and prediction. According to empiricism, to explain causally or predict a real phenomenon is to formulate a statement of either the type "if A, then B" or, should the variables allow quantitative measurement, "if an increase (decrease) in A, then an increase (decrease) in B."

As a statement referring to reality (with A and B being real phenomena), its validity can never be established with certainty, that is, by examining the proposition alone, or of any other proposition from which the one in question could be logically deduced. The statement will always be and always remain hypothetical, its veracity depending on the outcome of future observational experiences which cannot be known in advance. Should experience confirm a hypothetical causal explanation, this would not prove that the hypothesis was true. Should one observe an instance where B indeed followed A as predicted, it verifies nothing. A and B are general, abstract terms, or in philosophical terminology, universals, which refer to events and processes of which there are (or might be, in principle) an indefinite number of instances. Later experiences could still possibly falsify it.

d if an experience falsified a hypothesis, this would not be decisive either. For if it was observed that *A* was not followed by *B*, it would still be possible that the hypothetically related phenomena were causally linked. It could be that some other circumstance or variable, heretofore neglected and uncontrolled, had simply prevented the hypothesized relationship from actually being observed. At the most, falsification only proves that the particular hypothesis under investigation was not completely correct as it stood. It needs some refinement, some specification of additional variables which have to be watched for and controlled so that we might observe the hypothesized relationship between *A* and *B*. But, to be sure, a falsification would never prove once and for all that a relationship between some given phenomena did not exist, just as a confirmation would never definitively prove that it did exist.[21]

When we consider this position, we notice that it again implies a denial of a priori knowledge that is at the same time knowledge about anything real. Any proposition that claims to be a priori can, according to empiricism, be no more than signs on paper that are related to each other by definition or by arbitrary stipulation, and is thus completely void: it is without connection to the world of real things whatsoever. Such a system of signs only becomes an empirically meaningful theory once an empirical interpretation is given to its symbols. Yet as soon as such an interpretation is given to its symbols, the theory is no longer a priori true but rather becomes and remains forever hypothetical.

---

[21]On the relativistic and—on the level of politics—interventionist implications of empiricism, see Hans-Hermann Hoppe, "The Intellectual Cover for Socialism," *The Free Market* (February 1988).

Moreover, according to empiricism, we cannot know with certainty whether something is a possible cause of something else. If we want to explain some phenomenon, our hypothesizing about possible causes is in no way constrained by a priori considerations. Everything can have some influence on anything. We must find out by experience whether it does or not; but then experience will never give us a definite answer to this question either.

The next point brings us to our central topic of this section: the relationship between history and theory. We notice that according to empiricism there is no principal difference between historical and theoretical explanations. Every explanation is of the same type. In order to explain a phenomenon we hypothesize some other phenomenon as its cause and then see whether or not the hypothesized cause indeed preceded the effect in time. A distinction exists between a historical and a theoretical explanation only insofar as a historical explanation refers to events that already happened, something that lies in the past, whereas a theoretical explanation would be an explanation, or rather a prediction, of an effect that has not yet occurred. Structurally, though, there is no difference between such historical explanations and theoretical predictions. There is, however, a pragmatic difference which explains why empiricists in particular stress the importance of a theory's predictive power and are not content with testing it only *vis-à-vis* historical data.[22] The reason for this is quite evident to anyone who was ever engaged in the foolish game of data analyses. If the phenomenon to be explained has already occurred, it is easy as cake to

---

[22]For the emphasis placed on prediction by empiricist–positivists, see in particular Milton Friedman, "The Methodology of Positive Economics" in Friedman, *Essays in Positive Economics* (Chicago: University of Chicago Press, 1953).

find all sorts of events that preceded it in time and could possibly be considered its cause. Moreover, if we don't want to lengthen our list of possible causes by finding more preceding variables, we can do the following (and in the age of computers, it's even easier): We can take any one of the preceding variables and try out different functional relationships between it and the variable to be explained—linear or curvilinear ones, recursive or non-recursive functions, additive or multiplicative relations, etc. Then one, two, three, we find what we were looking for: a functional relationship that fits the data. And you will find not just one but any amount of them that you could possibly desire.

But which of all these preceding events, or of all the types of relationships, is the cause or the causally effective relation? There are no a priori considerations, according to empiricism, that could help us here. And that, then, is the reason why empiricists emphasize the importance of predictions. In order to find out which one of these manifold historical explanations is indeed correct—or at least not false—we are asked to try them out by using them in predicting events that have not yet occurred, see how good they are, and thereby weed out the wrong explanations.

So much for empiricism and its ideas about theory, history, and forecasting. I will not go into a detailed analysis of the question whether or not this emphasis on predictive success changes much, if anything at all, with respect to the rather evident relativistic implications of empiricism. Just recall that according to its very own doctrine, neither a predictive confirmation nor a predictive falsification would help us either in deciding whether a causal relationship between a pair of variables did or did not exist. This should make it appear rather doubtful that anything is gained by making prediction the cornerstone of one's philosophy.

I would like to challenge the very starting point of the empiricists' philosophy. There are several conclusive refutations of empiricism. I will show the empiricist distinction between empirical and analytical knowledge to be plainly false and self-contradictory.[23] That will then lead us to developing the Austrian position on theory, history, and forecasting.

This is empiricism's central claim: Empirical knowledge must be verifiable or falsifiable by experience; and analytical knowledge, which is not so verifiable or falsifiable, thus cannot contain any empirical knowledge. If this is true, then it is fair to ask: What then is the status of this fundamental statement of empiricism? Evidently it must be either analytical or empirical.

Let us first assume it is analytical. According to the empiricist doctrine, however, an analytical proposition is nothing but scribbles on paper, hot air, entirely void of any meaningful content. It says nothing about anything real. And hence one would have to conclude that empiricism could not even say and mean what it seems to say and mean. Yet if, on the other hand, it says and means what we thought it did all along, then it *does* inform us about something real. As a matter of fact, it informs us about the fundamental structure of reality. It says that there is nothing in reality that can be known to be one way or another prior to future experiences which may confirm or disconfirm our hypothesis.

And if this meaningful proposition is taken to be analytical, that is, as a statement that does not allow any falsification and whose truth can be established by an analysis of

[23]On rationalist critiques of empiricism, see Kambartel, *Erfahrung und Struktur*; Brand Blanshard, *Reason and Analysis* (LaSalle, Ill.: Open Court, 1964); A. Pap, *Semantics and Necessary Truth* (New Haven, Conn.: Yale University Press, 1958); Martin Hollis and Edward Nell, *Rational Economic Man* (Cambridge: Cambridge University Press, 1975).

its terms alone, one has no less than a glaring contradiction at hand. Empiricism itself would prove to be nothing but self-defeating nonsense.[24]

So perhaps we should choose the other available option and declare the fundamental empiricist distinction between empirical and analytical knowledge an empirical statement. But then the empiricist position would no longer carry any weight whatsoever. For if this were done, it would have to be admitted that the proposition—as an empirical one—might well be wrong and that one would be entitled to hear on the basis of what criterion one would have to decide whether or not it was. More decisively, as an empirical proposition, right or wrong, it could only state a historical fact, something like "all heretofore scrutinized propositions fall indeed into the two categories analytical and empirical." The statement would be entirely irrelevant for determining whether it would be possible to produce propositions that are true a priori and are still empirical ones. Indeed, if empiricism's central claim were declared an empirical proposition, empiricism would cease altogether to be an epistemology, a logic of science, and would be no more than a completely arbitrary verbal convention of calling certain arbitrary ways of dealing with certain statements certain arbitrary names. Empiricism would be a position void of any justification.

---

[24]Writes Mises in *The Ultimate Foundation of Economic Science*:

> The essence of logical positivism is to deny the cognitive value of a priori knowledge by pointing out that all a priori propositions are merely analytic. They do not provide new information, but are merely verbal or tautological, asserting what has already been implied in the definitions and premises. Only experience can lead to synthetic propositions. There is an obvious objection against this doctrine, viz., that this proposition that there are no synthetic a priori propositions is in itself —as the present writer thinks, false—a synthetic a priori proposition, for it can manifestly not be established by experience. (p. 5)

What does this first step in our criticism of empiricism prove? It proves evidently that the empiricist idea of knowledge is wrong, and it proves this by means of a meaningful a priori argument. And in doing this, it shows that the Kantian and Misesian idea of true a priori synthetic propositions is correct. More specifically, it proves that the relationship between theory and history cannot be as depicted by empiricism. There must also be a realm of theory—theory that is empirically meaningful—which is categorically different from the only idea of theory empiricism admits to having existence. There must also be a priori theories, and the relationship between theory and history then must be different and more complicated than empiricism would have us believe. How different indeed will become apparent when I present another argument against empiricism, another a priori argument, and an a priori argument against the thesis implied in empiricism that the relation between theory and empirical research is the same in every field of knowledge.

However appropriate the empiricist ideas may be in dealing with the natural sciences (and I think they are inappropriate even there, but I cannot go into this here),[25] it is impossible to think that the methods of empiricism can be applicable in the social sciences.

Actions are the field of phenomena which constitutes what we regard as the subject matter of the social sciences. Empiricism claims that actions can and must be

---

[25]On this see, in addition to the works cited in note 23, in particular H. Dingler, *Die Ergreifung des Wirklichen* (Munich: 1955); idem, *Aufbau der exakten Fundamentalwissenschaft* (Münich: 1964; Paul Lorenzen, *Methodisches Denken* (Frankfurt/M.: 1968); F. Kambartel and J. Mittelstrass, eds., *Zum normativen Fundament der Wissenschaft* (Frankfurt/M.: 1973); also my "In Defense of Extreme Rationalism."

explained, just as any other phenomenon, by means of causal hypotheses which can be confirmed or falsified by experience.[26]

Now if this were the case, then empiricism would be first forced to assume—contrary to its own doctrine that no a priori knowledge about anything real exists—that time-invariantly operating causes with respect to actions exist.

One would not know a priori which particular event might be the cause of any particular action. But empiricism wants us to relate different experiences regarding sequences of events as either confirming or falsifying each other. And if they falsify each other, then we are to respond with a reformulation of the original hypothesis. Yet in order to do so, we must assume a constancy over time in the operation of causes as such—and to know that causes for actions do exist is, of course, knowledge about the reality of actions. Without such an assumption regarding the existence of causes as such, different experiences can never be related to each other as confirming or falsifying one another. They are simply unrelated, incommensurable observations. Here is one, there is another; they are the same or similar; or they are different. Nothing else follows.[27]

In addition, there is yet another contradiction, and making it evident will immediately lead us to Mises's central

[26]In addition to the literature cited in note 20 see, for instance, such typical empiricist products as Arthur Goldberger and Otis D. Duncan, eds., *Structural Equation Models in the Social Sciences* (San Diego, Calif.: Academic Press, 1973); H. B. Blalock, ed., *Causal Inferences in Non-Experimental Research* (Chapel Hill: University of North Carolina Press, 1964); Arthur L. Stinchcombe, *Constructing Social Theories* (New York: Harcourt, Brace & World, 1968).

[27]On this and the following, see Hoppe, *Kritik der kausalwissenschaftlichen Sozialforschung*, chapter 2, and "Is Research Based on Causal Scientific Principles Possible in the Social Sciences?"

insight that the relationship between theory and history in the field of the social sciences is of an entirely different nature than that in the natural sciences.

What is this contradiction? If actions could indeed be conceived of as governed by time-invariantly operating causes, then it is certainly appropriate to ask: But what then about explaining the explainers? What about causally predicting their actions? They are, after all, the persons who carry on the very process of creating hypotheses and of verification and falsification.

In order to assimilate confirming or falsifying experiences—to replace old hypotheses with new ones—one must assumedly be able to learn from experience. Every empiricist is, of course, forced to admit this. Otherwise why engage in empirical research at all?

But if one can learn from experience in as yet unknown ways, then one admittedly cannot know at any given time what one will know at a later time and, accordingly, how one will act on the basis of this knowledge. One can only reconstruct the causes of one's actions after the event, as one can explain one's knowledge only after one already possesses it. Indeed, no scientific advance could ever alter the fact that one must regard one's knowledge and actions as unpredictable on the basis of constantly operating causes. One might hold this conception of freedom to be an illusion. And one might well be correct from the point of view of a scientist with cognitive powers substantially superior to any human intelligence, or from the point of view of God. But we are not God, and even if our freedom is illusory from His standpoint and our actions follow a predictable path, for us this is a necessary and unavoidable illusion. We cannot predict in advance, on the basis of our previous states, the future states of our knowledge or the actions manifesting that knowledge. We can only reconstruct them after the event.[28]

Thus, the empiricist methodology is simply contradictory when applied to the field of knowledge and action—which contains knowledge as its necessary ingredient. The empiricist-minded social scientists who formulate prediction equations regarding social phenomena are simply doing nonsense. Their activity of engaging in an enterprise whose outcome they must admit they do not yet know, proves that what they pretend to do cannot be done. As Mises puts it and has emphasized repeatedly: There are no empirical causal constants in the field of human action.[29]

By means of a priori reasoning then, one has established this insight: Social history, as opposed to natural history, does not yield any knowledge that can be employed for predictive purposes. Rather, social and economic history refers exclusively to the past. The outcome of research into how and why people acted in the past has no systematic bearing on whether or not they will act the same way in the future. People can learn. It is absurd to assume that one could predict in the present what one will know tomorrow and in what way tomorrow's knowledge will or will not be different from today's.

A person cannot predict today his demand for sugar in one year any more than Einstein could have predicted the

---

[28]Interestingly, this argument was first advanced by Karl R. Popper in the Preface to his *The Poverty of Historicism* (London: Routledge & Kegan Paul, 1957). However, Popper entirely failed to notice that such an argument actually invalidates his own idea of a methodological monism (*Einheitswissenschaft*) and demonstrates the inapplicability of his falsificationism in the field of human action and knowledge. See on this my *Kritik der kausalwissenschaftlichen Sozialforschung*, pp. 44–49; K. O. Apel, *Die Erklären: Verstehen Kontroverse in transzendental-pragmatischer Sicht* (Frankfurt/M.: 1979), pp. 44–46, footnote 19.

[29]Mises, *Human Action*, pp. 55–56.

---

theory of relativity before he had actually developed it. A person cannot know today what he will know about sugar one year from now. And he cannot know all the goods that will be competing against sugar for his money in a year. He can make a guess, of course. But since it must be admitted that future states of knowledge cannot be predicted on the basis of constantly operating causes, a person cannot pretend to make a prediction of the same epistemological type as, for instance, one regarding the future behavior of the moon, the weather, or the tides. Those are predictions that could legitimately make use of the assumption of time-invariantly operating causes. But a prediction about future sugar demand would be an entirely different thing.

Provided social and economic history can only come up with reconstructive explanations and never with explanations that have any systematic predictive relevance, another extremely important insight regarding the logic of empirical social research follows. And this amounts to another decisive criticism of empiricism, at least regarding its claim of being an appropriate methodology for social science research.

Recall what I said earlier about why it is that empiricism so strongly emphasizes the predictive function of explanatory theories. For every phenomenon to be explained there are a multitude of preceding events and a multitude of functional relationships with such preceding events by which the phenomenon in question could possibly be explained. But which of these rival explanations is correct and which ones are not? The empiricist answer was: Try to predict, and your success or failure in predicting future events will tell you which explanation is or is not correct. Evidently, this advice won't do if there are no time-invariantly operating causes with respect to actions. What then? Empiricism, of course, cannot have an answer to this question.

Yet even if actions cannot be predicted in any scientific way, this does not imply that one reconstructive historical explanation is just as good as any other. It would be regarded as absurd if someone explained the fact that I moved from Germany to the United States by pointing out, for example, that the corn in Michigan, prior to my decision, was experiencing a growth spurt and that this had caused my decision. But why not, assuming here that the event regarding Michigan's corn indeed happened prior to my decision? The reason is, of course, that I will tell you that Michigan's corn had no relevance for my decision. And insofar as anything is known about me at all, it can be recognized that this is indeed the case.

But how can you recognize this? The answer is by understanding my motives and interests, my convictions and aspirations, my normative orientations, and my concrete perceptions resulting in this action. How do we understand somebody and, moreover, how do we verify that our understanding is indeed correct? As regards the first part of the question—one understands somebody by engaging in a pseudo-communication and interaction with him. I say pseudo because, evidently, we cannot engage in an actual communication with Caesar in order to find out why he crossed the Rubicon. But we could study his writings and compare his convictions expressed therein with his actual deeds; we could study the writings and actions of contemporaries and thereby try to understand Caesar's personality, his time, and his particular role and position within his time.[30]

---

[30]On the logic of history, see Mises, *Theory and History*, chapter 14; *The Ultimate Foundation of Economic Science*, pp. 45–51; *Human Action*, pp. 47–51, 59–64.

As regards the second part of the question—the problem of verification of historical explanations—one has to admit from the outset that there is no absolutely clear-cut criterion that would allow one to decide which one of two rival explanations, both equally based on understanding, is definitely correct and which one is not. History is not an exact science in the same sense as the natural sciences are exact sciences or in the very different sense in which economics is an exact science.

Even if two historians agree in their description of facts and their assessment of factors of influence for a given action to be explained, they might still disagree on the weight that should be assigned to such factors in bringing about the action. And there would be no way to decide the matter in a completely unambiguous way.[31]

Yet let me not be misunderstood here. There is nonetheless some sort of truth-criterion for historical explanations. It is a criterion that does not eliminate all possible disagreements among historians, but that still excludes and disqualifies a wide range of explanations. The criterion is that any true historical explanation must be of such a kind that the actor whose actions are to be explained must, in principle, be able to verify the explanation and the explanatory factors as being those that contributed to his acting the way he did.[32] The key phrase here is: in principle. Naturally, Caesar could not possibly verify our explanation for his crossing the Rubicon. Moreover, he might actually have strong reasons not to verify the explanation even if he could, since such a verification might conflict with some other objectives that he might have.

---

[31]Mises, *Human Action*, pp. 57–58.

[32]On the logic of historical and sociological reconstruction and verification, see also Hoppe, *Kritik der kausalwissenschaftlichen Sozialforschung*, pp. 33–38.

Also, to say that any true explanation must be verifiable by the actor in question is not to say that every actor is always best qualified to be his own explainer. It may be that Einstein can explain better than anyone else why and how he came up with the theory of relativity when he did. But this might not be so. As a matter of fact, it may well be possible that a historian of science may understand Einstein and the influences leading to his discovery better than he himself did or could. And this would be possible because the influencing factors or the rules that determined one's actions might only be subconscious.[33] Or they might be so obvious that one would fail to notice them simply on account of this.

The following analogy may be quite helpful in understanding the curious fact that others might understand a person better than the person himself. Take, for example, a public speech. Of course, to a large extent the person giving the speech can probably give reasons for saying what he says and formulate the influences that led him to see things the way he does. He can probably do so better than anyone else. And yet, in saying what he says, he follows rules habitually and unconsciously that he could hardly or only with great difficulties make explicit. He also follows certain rules of grammar when he says what he says. But quite often he would be completely unable to formulate these rules even though they clearly influence his actions. The historian who understands someone's actions better than the person himself is quite analogous to the grammarian analyzing the sentence structure of the public speaker. Both reconstruct

---

[33]On the logic of psychoanalytic explanation and verification, see A. MacIntyre, *The Unconscious* (London: Duckworth, 1958); Jürgen Habermas, *Erkenntnis und Interesse* (Frankfurt/M.: 1968), chapter 2; on the relevance of psychoanalysis also Mises, *Human Action*, p. 12.

and explicitly formulate the rules that are actually followed, but that could not, or only with extreme difficulties, be formulated by the speaker himself.[34]

The speaker may not be able to formulate all the rules that he follows and may need the professional historian or grammarian to help him. But it is of great importance to realize that the truth criterion for the grammarian's explanation would nonetheless be that the speaker would have to be able—in principle—to verify the correctness of the explanation after what was previously known implicitly was made explicit. In order for the grammarian's or historian's explanations to be correct, the actor would need to be able to recognize these rules as being those which indeed influenced his actions. So much for the logic of historical research as necessarily reconstructive research based on understanding.[35]

The argument establishing the impossibility of causal predictions in the field of human knowledge and actions now might have left the impression that if this is so, then forecasting can be nothing but successful or unsuccessful guessing. This impression, however, would be just as wrong

---

[34]On the logic of linguistic explanations as involving the reconstruction of rules which require confirmation through the "intuitive knowledge" of "competent speakers," see Noam Chomsky, *Aspects of the Theory of Syntax* (Cambridge: M.I.T. Press, 1965); also K. O. Apel, "Noam Chomskys Sprachtheorie und die Philosophie der Gegenwart" in Apel, *Transformation der Philosophie*, vol. 2 (Frankfurt/M.: 1973).

[35]For important critiques of the empiricist–positivist philosophy of the empirical social sciences, and explanations of social research as based on reconstructive understanding, see also K. O. Apel, *Transformation der Philosophie*; idem, *Die Erklären: Verstehen Kontroverse in transzendental-pragmatischer Sicht*; Peter Winch, *The Idea of a Social Science and Its Relation to Philosophy* (Atlantic Highlands, N.J.: Humanities Press, 1970); idem, *Ethics and Action* (London: Routledge and Kegan Paul, 1972); Jürgen Habermas, *Zur Logik der Sozialwissenschaften* (Frankfurt/M.: 1970); G. H. von Wright, *Explanation and Understanding* (Ithaca, N.Y.: Cornell University Press, 1971).

---

as it would be wrong to think that one can predict human action in the same way as one can predict the growing stages of apples. It is here where the unique Misesian insight into the interplay of economic theory and history enters the picture.[36]

In fact, the reason why the social and economic future cannot be regarded as entirely and absolutely uncertain should not be too hard to understand: The impossibility of causal predictions in the field of action was proven by means of an a priori argument. And this argument incorporated a priori true knowledge about actions as such: that they cannot be conceived of as governed by time-invariantly operating causes.

Thus, while economic forecasting will indeed always be a systematically unteachable art, it is at the same time true that all economic forecasts must be thought of as being constrained by the existence of a priori knowledge about actions as such.[37]

Take, for example, the quantity theory of money, the praxeological proposition that if you increase the quantity

---

[36]On the relation between theory and history, see in particular Mises, *Human Action*, pp. 51–59; and *Epistemological Problems of Economics*, chapters 2–3.

[37]The former Austrian and neo-historicist–hermeneutician–nihilist Ludwig Lachmann, who repeats *ad nauseam* the unpredictability of future states of knowledge (see his "From Mises to Shackle: An Essay on Austrian Economics and the Kaleidic Society," *Journal of Economic Literature* 54 (1976); *The Market as an Economic Process* (New York: Basil Blackwell, 1986), entirely misses recognizing this latter point. In fact, his arguments are simply self-defeating. For evidently he claims to know for certain the unknowability of future knowledge and, by logical extension, of actions. Yet then he does know something about future knowledge and action. He must know something about knowledge and action as such. And this, precisely, is what praxeology claims to be: knowledge regarding actions as such, and (as I have explained in my "On Praxeology and the Praxeological Foundations of Epistemology and Ethics," p. 49 below) knowledge about the structure which any future knowledge must have by virtue of the fact that it invariably must be knowledge of actors.

of money and the demand for money stays constant, then the purchasing power of money will fall. Our a priori knowledge about actions as such informs us that it is impossible to predict scientifically whether or not the quantity of money will be increased, decreased or left unchanged. Nor is it possible to predict scientifically whether or not, regardless of what happens to the quantity of money, the demand for money to be held in cash balances will go up or down or stay the same. We cannot claim to be able to predict such things because we cannot predict future states of knowledge of people. And yet these states evidently influence what happens with respect to the quantity of money and the demand for money. Then, our theory, our praxeological knowledge incorporated in the quantity theory, has a rather limited usefulness for one's business of predicting the economic future.

The theory would not allow one to predict future economic events even if, say, it is an established fact that the quantity of money had been expanded. One would still be unable to predict what would happen to the demand for money. And though, of course, concurrent events regarding the demand for money do affect the shape of things to come (and cancel, increase, decrease, accelerate, or decelerate the effects stemming from the source of an increased money supply), such concurrent changes cannot in principle be predicted or experimentally held constant. It is an outright absurdity to conceive of subjective knowledge, whose every change has an impact on actions, as predictable on the basis of antecedent variables and as capable of being held constant. The very experimenter who wanted to hold knowledge constant would, in fact, have to presuppose that his knowledge, specifically his knowledge regarding the experiment's outcome, could not be assumed to be constant over time.

The quantity theory of money then cannot render any specific economic event, certain or probable, on the basis of a formula employing prediction constants. However, the theory would nonetheless restrict the range of possibly correct predictions. And it would do this not as an empirical theory, but rather as a praxeological theory, acting as a logical constraint on our prediction-making.[38] Predictions that are not in line with such knowledge (in our case: the quantity theory) are systematically flawed and making them leads to systematically increasing numbers of forecasting errors. This does not mean that someone who based his predictions on correct praxeological reasoning would necessarily have to be a better predictor of future economic events than someone who arrived at his predictions through logically flawed deliberations and chains of reasoning. It means that in the long run the praxeologically enlightened forecaster would average better than the unenlightened ones.

It is possible to make the wrong prediction in spite of the fact that one has correctly identified the event "increase in the money supply" and in spite of one's praxeologically correct reasoning that such an event is by logical necessity connected with the event "drop in the purchasing power of money." For one might go wrong predicting what will occur to the event "demand for money." One may have predicted a constant demand for money, but the demand might actually increase. Thus the predicted inflation might not show up as expected. And on the other hand, it is equally possible that a person could make a correct forecast, i.e., there will be no drop in purchasing power, in spite of the fact that he

---

[38]On the logic of social and economic forecasting, see also Hoppe, "In Defense of Extreme Rationalism," sections 3, 4.

was wrongly convinced that a rise in the quantity of money had nothing to do with money's purchasing power. For it may be that another concurrent change occurred (the demand for money increased) which counteracted his wrong assessment of causes and consequences and accidentally happened to make his prediction right.

However, and this brings me back to my point that praxeology logically constrains our predictions of economic events: What if we assume that all forecasters, including those with and without sound praxeological knowledge, are on the average equally well-equipped to anticipate other concurrent changes? What if they are on the average equally lucky guessers of the social and economic future? Evidently, we must conclude then that forecasters making predictions in recognition of and in accordance with praxeological laws like the quantity theory of money will be more successful than that group of forecasters which is ignorant of praxeology.

It is impossible to build a prediction formula which employs the assumption of time-invariantly operating causes that would enable us to scientifically forecast changes in the demand for money. The demand for money is necessarily dependent on people's future states of knowledge, and future knowledge is unpredictable. And thus praxeological knowledge has very limited predictive utility.[39]

Yet of all forecasters who correctly forecast that a change such as an increase in the demand for money will take place and who equally correctly perceive that an increase in the

---

[39] See also Murray N. Rothbard, *Power and Market* (Kansas City, Kans.: Sheed Andrews and McMeel, 1977), pp. 256–58, on the different function of economic theorizing in a free market environment vs. an environment hampered by government intervention.

quantity of money has indeed happened, only those who recognize the quantity theory of money will make a correct prediction. And those whose convictions are at variance with praxeology will necessarily go wrong.

To understand the logic of economic forecasting and the practical function of praxeological reasoning, then, is to view the a priori theorems of economics as acting as logical constraints on empirical predictions and as imposing logical limits on what can or cannot happen in the future.

ON PRAXEOLOGY
AND THE PRAXEOLOGICAL
FOUNDATION OF EPISTEMOLOGY

I

As have most great and innovative economists, Ludwig von Mises intensively and repeatedly analyzed the problem of the logical status of economic propositions, i.e., how we come to know them and how we validate them. Indeed, Mises ranks foremost among those who hold that such a concern is indispensable in order to achieve systematic progress in economics. For any misconception regarding the answer to such fundamental questions of one's intellectual enterprise would naturally have to lead to intellectual disaster, i.e., to false economic doctrines. Accordingly, three of Mises's books are devoted entirely to clarifying the logical foundations of economics: His early *Epistemological Problems of Economics*, published in German in 1933; his *Theory and History* of 1957; and his *Ultimate Foundations of Economic Science* of 1962, Mises's last book, appearing when he was already well past his eightieth birthday. And his works in the field of economics proper also invariably display the importance which Mises attached to the analysis of epistemological

This essay is from Hans-Hermann Hoppe, *The Economics and Ethics of Private Property* (Kluwer Academic Publishers in 1993), pp. 141–64 and it is reprinted here with permission of Kluwer Academic Publishers.

problems. Most characteristically, *Human Action*, his master-piece, deals in its first hundred-odd pages exclusively with such problems, and the other nearly 800 pages of the book are permeated with epistemological considerations.

Quite in line with the tradition of Mises, then, the foundations of economics are also the subject of this chapter. I have set myself a twofold goal. First, I want to explain the solution which Mises advances regarding the problem of the ultimate foundation of economic science, i.e., his idea of a pure theory of action, or praxeology, as he himself terms it. And secondly, I want to demonstrate why Mises's solution is much more than just an incontestable insight into the nature of economics and economic propositions.

It provides an insight that also enables us to understand the foundation on which epistemology ultimately rests. In fact, as the title of the chapter suggests, I want to show that it is praxeology which must be regarded as the very foundation of epistemology, and hence that Mises, aside from his great achievements as an economist, also contributed path-breaking insights regarding the justification of the entire enterprise of rationalist philosophy.[40]

II

Let me turn to Mises's solution. What is the logical status of typical economic propositions such as the law of marginal utility (that whenever the supply of a good whose

[40]See on the following also my *Kritik der kausalwissenschaftlichen Sozialfor-schung. Untersuchungen zur Grundlegung von Soziologie und Ökonomie*; idem, "Is Research Based on Causal Scientific Principles Possible in the Social Sciences?," chapter 7); idem, "In Defense of Extreme Rationalism."

units are regarded as of equal serviceability by a person increases by one additional unit, the value attached to this unit must decrease as it can only be employed as a means for the attainment of a goal that is considered less valuable than the least valuable goal previously satisfied by a unit of this good); or of the quantity theory of money (that whenever the quantity of money is increased while the demand for money to be held in cash reserve on hand is unchanged, the purchasing power of money will fall)?

In formulating his answer, Mises faced a double challenge. On the one hand, there was the answer offered by modern empiricism. The Vienna Ludwig von Mises knew was in fact one of the early centers of the empiricist movement: a movement which was then on the verge of establishing itself as the dominant academic philosophy of the Western world for several decades, and which to this very day shapes the image that an overwhelming majority of economists have of their own discipline.[41]

Empiricism considers nature and the natural sciences as its model. According to empiricism, the aforementioned examples of economic propositions have the same logical

---

[41]On the Vienna Circle see V. Kraft, *Der Wiener Kreis* (Vienna: Springer, 1968); for empiricist–positivist interpretations of economics see such representative works as Terence W. Hutchison, *The Significance and Basic Postulates of Economic Theory* [Hutchison, an adherent of the Popperian variant of empiricism, has since become much less enthusiastic about the prospects of a Popperized economics—see, for instance, his *Knowledge and Ignorance in Economics*—yet he still sees no alternative but to cling to Popper's falsificationism anyway.]; Milton Friedman, "The Methodology of Positive Economics," in idem, *Essays in Positive Economics*; Mark Blaug, *The Methodology of Economics*; a positivist account by a participant in Mises's *Privat Seminar* in Vienna is F. Kaufmann, *Methodology of the Social Sciences*; the dominance of empiricism in economics is documented by the fact that there is probably not a single textbook, which does not explicitly classify economics as—what else?—an empirical (a posteriori) science.

status as laws of nature: Like laws of nature they state hypothetical relationships between two or more events, essentially in the form of if-then statements. And like hypotheses of the natural sciences, the propositions of economics require continual testing *vis-à-vis* experience. A proposition regarding the relationship between economic events can never be validated once and for all with certainty. Instead, it is forever subject to the outcome of contingent, future experiences. Such experience might confirm the hypothesis. But this would not prove the hypothesis to be true, since the economic proposition would have used general terms (in philosophical terminology: universals) in its description of the related events, and thus would apply to an indefinite number of cases or instances, thereby always leaving room for possibly falsifying future experiences. All a confirmation would prove is that the hypothesis had not yet turned out wrong. On the other hand, the experience might falsify the hypothesis. This would surely prove that something was wrong with the hypothesis as it stood. But it would not prove that the hypothesized relationship between the specified events could never be observed. It would merely show that considering and controlling in one's observations only what up to now had been actually accounted for and controlled, the relationship had not yet shown up. It cannot be ruled out, however, that it might show up as soon as some other circumstances have been controlled.

The attitude that this philosophy fuels and that has indeed become characteristic of most contemporary economists and their way of conducting their business is one of skepticism: the motto being "nothing can be known with certainty to be impossible in the realm of economic phenomena." Even more precisely, since empiricism conceives of economic phenomena as objective data, extending in space and subject to quantifiable measurement—in strict analogy to the phenomena of the natural sciences—the peculiar skepticism of the empiricist economist may be described as that of a social engineer who will not guarantee anything.[42]

The other challenge came from the side of the historicist school. Indeed, during Mises's life in Austria and Switzerland, the historicist philosophy was the prevailing ideology of the German-speaking universities and their establishment. With the upsurge of empiricism this former prominence has been reduced considerably. But over roughly the last decade historicism has regained momentum among the Western world's academia. Today it is with us everywhere under the names of hermeneutics, rhetoric, deconstructionism, and epistemological anarchism.[43]

For historicism, and most conspicuously for its contemporary versions, the model is not nature but a literary text. Economic phenomena, according to the historicist doctrine, are not objective magnitudes that can be measured. Instead, they are subjective expressions and interpretations unfolding in history to be understood and interpreted by the economist

[42]On the relativistic consequences of empiricism–positivism see also Hoppe, *A Theory of Socialism and Capitalism* (Boston: Kluwer Academic Publishers, 1989), chapter 6; idem, "The Intellectual Cover for Socialism."

[43]See Ludwig von Mises, *The Historical Setting of the Austrian School of Economics* (Auburn, Ala.:Ludwig von Mises Institute, 1984); idem, *Erinnerungen* (Stuttgart: Gustav Fischer, 1978); idem, *Theory and History*, chapter 10; Murray N. Rothbard, *Ludwig von Mises: Scholar, Creator, Hero* (Auburn, Ala.: Ludwig von Mises Institute, 1988); for a critical survey of historicist ideas see also Karl Popper, *The Poverty of Historicism*; for a representative of the older version of a historicist interpretation of economics see Werner Sombart, *Die drei Nationalökonomien* (Munich: Duncker & Humblot, 1930); for the modern, hermeneutical twist Donald McCloskey, *The Rhetoric of Economics* (Madison: University of Wisconsin Press, 1985); Ludwig Lachmann, "From Mises to Shackle: An Essay on Austrian Economics and the Kaleidic Society," *Journal of Economic Literature* (1976).

just as a literary text unfolds before and is interpreted by its reader. As subjective creations, the sequence of their events follows no objective law. Nothing in the literary text, and nothing in the sequence of historical expressions and interpretations is governed by constant relations. Of course, certain literary texts actually exist, and so do certain sequences of historical events. But this by no means implies that anything had to happen in the order it did. It simply occurred. In the same way, however, as one can always invent different literary stories, history and the sequence of historical events, too, might have happened in an entirely different way. Moreover, according to historicism, and particularly visible in its modern hermeneutical version, the formation of these always contingently related human expressions and their interpretations is also not constrained by any objective law. In literary production anything can be expressed or interpreted concerning everything; and, along the same line, historical and economic events are whatever someone expresses or interprets them to be, and their description by the historian and economist is then whatever he expresses or interprets these past subjective events to have been.

The attitude that historicist philosophy generates is one of relativism. Its motto is "everything is possible." Unconstrained by any objective law, for the historicist–hermeneutician history and economics, along with literary criticism, are matters of esthetics. And accordingly, his output takes on the form of disquisitions on what someone feels about what he feels was felt by somebody else—a literary form which we are only too familiar with, in particular in such fields as sociology and political science.[44]

---

[44]On the extreme relativism of historicism–hermeneutics see Hoppe, "In Defense of Extreme Rationalism"; Murray N. Rothbard, "The Hermeneutical Invasion of Philosophy and Economics," *Review of Austrian Economics* (1988); Henry Veatch,

I trust that one senses intuitively that something is seriously amiss in both the empiricist as well as the historicist philosophies. Their epistemological accounts do not even seem to fit their own self-chosen models: nature on the one hand and literary texts on the other. And in any case, regarding economic propositions such as the law of marginal utility or the quantity theory of money their accounts seem to be simply wrong. The law of marginal utility certainly does not strike one as a hypothetical law subject forever for its validation to confirming or disconfirming experiences popping up here or there. And to conceive of the phenomena talked about in the law as quantifiable magnitudes seems to be nothing but ridiculous. Nor does the historicist interpretation seem to be any better. To think that the relationship between the events referred to in the quantity theory of money can be undone if one only wished to do so seems absurd. And the idea appears no less absurd that concepts such as money, demand for money, and purchasing power are formed without any objective constraints and refer merely to whimsical subjective creations. Instead, contrary to the empiricist doctrine, both examples of economic propositions appear to be logically true and to refer to events which are subjective in nature. And contrary to historicism, it would seem that what they state, then, could not possibly be undone in all of history and would contain conceptual distinctions which, while referring to subjective events, were nonetheless objectively constrained, and would incorporate universally valid knowledge.

"Deconstruction in Philosophy: Has Rorty Made it the Denouement of Contemporary Analytical Philosophy," *Review of Metaphysics* (1985); Jonathan Barnes, "A Kind of Integrity," *Austrian Economics Newsletter* (Summer 1987); David Gordon, *Hermeneutics vs. Austrian Economics* (Auburn, Ala.: Ludwig von Mises Institute, Occasional Paper Series, 1987); for a brilliant critique of contemporary sociology see St. Andreski, *Social Science as Sorcery* (New York: St. Martin's Press, 1973).

Like most of the better known economists before him, Mises shares these intuitions.[45] Yet in quest of the foundation of economics, Mises goes beyond intuition. He takes on the challenge posed by empiricism and historicism in order to reconstruct systematically the basis on which these intuitions can be understood as correct and justified. He thereby does not want to help bring about a new discipline of economics. But in explaining what formerly had only been grasped intuitively, Mises goes far beyond what had ever been done before. In reconstructing the rational foundations of the economists' intuitions, he assures us of the proper path for any future development in economics and safeguards us against systematic intellectual error.

Empiricism and historicism, Mises notes at the outset of his reconstruction, are self-contradictory doctrines.[46] The empiricist notion that all events, natural or economic, are only hypothetically related is contradicted by the message of this very basic empiricist proposition itself: For if this proposition were regarded as itself being merely hypothetically true, i.e., a hypothetically true proposition regarding hypothetically true propositions, it would not even qualify as an epistemological pronouncement. For it would then provide no justification whatsoever for the claim that economic

[45] Regarding the epistemological views of such predecessors as J. B. Say, Nassau W. Senior, J. E. Cairnes, John Stuart Mill, Carl Menger, and Friedrich von Wieser see Ludwig von Mises, *Epistemological Problems of Economics*, pp. 17–23; also Murray N. Rothbard, "Praxeology: The Methodology of Austrian Economics," in Edwin Dolan, ed., *The Foundations of Modern Austrian Economics* (Kansas City: Sheed and Ward, 1976).

[46] In addition to Mises's works cited at the outset of this chapter and the literature mentioned in note 40, see Murray N. Rothbard, *Individualism and the Philosophy of the Social Sciences* (San Francisco: Cato Institute, 1979); for a splendid philosophical critique of empiricist economics see Hollis and Nell, *Rational Economic Man*; as particularly valuable general defenses of rationalism as against empiricism and relativism—without reference to economics, however,—see Blanshard, *Reason and Analysis*; Kambartel, *Erfahrung und Struktur*.

propositions are not, and cannot be, categorically, or a priori true, as our intuition informs us they are. If, however, the basic empiricist premise were assumed to be categorically true itself, i.e., if we assume that one could say something a priori true about the way events are related, then this would belie its very own thesis that empirical knowledge must invariably be hypothetical knowledge, thus making room for a discipline such as economics claiming to produce a priori valid empirical knowledge. Further, the empiricist thesis that economic phenomena must be conceived of as observable and measurable magnitudes—analogous to those of the natural sciences—is rendered inconclusive, too, on its own account: For, obviously, empiricism wants to provide us with meaningful empirical knowledge when it informs us that our economic concepts are grounded in observations. And yet, the concepts of observation and measurement themselves, which empiricism must employ in claiming what it does, are both obviously not derived from observational experience in the sense that concepts such as hens and eggs or apples and pears are. One cannot observe someone making an observation or measurement. Rather, one must first understand what observations and measurements are in order to then be able to interpret certain observable phenomena as the making of an observation or the taking of a measurement. Thus, contrary to its own doctrine, empiricism is compelled to admit that there is empirical knowledge which is based on understanding—just as according to our intuitions economic propositions claim to be based on understanding—rather than on observations.[47]

[47]For an elaborate defense of epistemological dualism see also Apel, *Transformation der Philosophie,* 2 vols. and Habermas, *Zur Logik der Sozialwissenschaften.*

And regarding historicism, its self-contradictions are no less manifest. For if, as historicism claims, historical and economic events—which it conceives of as sequences of subjectively understood rather than observed events—are not governed by any constant, time-invariant relations, then this very proposition also cannot claim to say anything constantly true about history and economics. Instead, it would be a proposition with, so to speak, a fleeting truth value: it may be true now, if we wish it so, yet possibly false a moment later, in case we do not, with no one ever knowing anything about whether we do or do not. Yet, if this were the status of the basic historicist premise, it, too, would obviously not qualify as an epistemology. Historicism would not have given us any reason why we should believe any of it. If, however, the basic proposition of historicism were assumed to be invariantly true, then such a proposition about the constant nature of historical and economic phenomena would contradict its own doctrine denying any such constants. Furthermore, the historicist's—and even more so its modern heir, the hermeneutician's—claim that historical and economic events are mere subjective creations, unconstrained by any objective factors, is proven false by the very statement making it. For evidently, a historicist must assume this very statement to be meaningful and true; he must presume to say something specific about something, rather than merely uttering meaningless sounds like abracadabra. Yet if this is the case, then, clearly, his statement must be assumed to be constrained by something outside the realm of arbitrary subjective creations. Of course, I can say what the historicist says in English, German, or Chinese, or in any other language I wish, in so far as historic and economic expressions and interpretations may well be regarded as mere subjective creations. But whatever I say in whatever language I choose must be assumed to be constrained by some underlying propositional meaning of my statement, which is the same for any language, and exists completely independent of whatever the peculiar linguistic form may be in which it is expressed. And contrary to historicist belief, the existence of such a constraint is not such that one could possibly dispose of it at will. Rather, it is objective in that we can understand it to be the logically necessary presupposition for saying anything meaningful at all, as opposed to merely producing meaningless sounds. The historicist could not claim to say anything if it were not for the fact that his expressions and interpretations are actually constrained by laws of logic as the very presupposition of meaningful statements as such.[48]

With such a refutation of empiricism and historicism, Mises notices, the claims of rationalist philosophy are successfully reestablished, and the case is made for the possibility of a priori true statements, as those of economics seem to be. Indeed, Mises explicitly regards his own epistemological investigations as the continuation of the work of western rationalist philosophy. With Leibniz and Kant he stands opposite the tradition of Locke and Hume.[49] He sides with Leibniz when he answers Locke's famous dictum "nothing is in the intellect that has not previously been in the senses" with his equally famous one "except the intellect itself." And he recognizes his task as a philosopher of economics as strictly analogous to that of Kant's as a philosopher of pure reason, i.e., of epistemology. Like Kant, Mises wants to demonstrate the existence of true a priori synthetic propositions, or propositions whose truth values can be definitely established, even

---

[48]See on this in particular Hoppe, "In Defense of Extreme Rationalism."

[49]See Mises, *The Ultimate Foundation of Economic Science*, p. 12.

though in order to do so the means of formal logic are insufficient and observations are unnecessary.

My criticism of empiricism and historicism has proved the general rationalist claim. It has proved that we indeed do possess knowledge which is not derived from observation and yet is constrained by objective laws. In fact, our refutation of empiricism and historicism contains such a priori synthetic knowledge. Yet what about the constructive task of showing that the propositions of economics—such as the law of marginal utility and the quantity theory of money—qualify as this type of knowledge? In order to do so, Mises notices in accordance with the strictures traditionally formulated by rationalist philosophers, economic propositions must fulfill two requirements: First, it must be possible to demonstrate that they are not derived from observational evidence, for observational evidence can only reveal things as they happen to be; there is nothing in it that would indicate why things *must* be the way they are. Instead, economic propositions must be shown to be grounded in reflective cognition, in our understanding of ourselves as knowing subjects. And secondly, this reflective understanding must yield certain propositions as self-evident material axioms. Not in the sense that such axioms would have to be self-evident in a psychological sense, that is, that one would have to be immediately aware of them or that their truth depends on a psychological feeling of conviction. On the contrary, like Kant before him, Mises very much stresses the fact that it is usually much more painstaking to discover such axioms than it is to discover some observational truth such as that the leaves of trees are green or that I am 6 foot 2 inches.[50] Rather, what

---

[50]See Kant, *Kritik der reinen Vernunft*, p. 45; Mises, *Human Action*, p. 38.

makes them self-evident material axioms is the fact that no one can deny their validity without self-contradiction, because in attempting to deny them one already presupposes their validity.

Mises points out that both requirements are fulfilled by what he terms the axiom of action, i.e., the proposition that humans act, that they display intentional behavior.[51] Obviously, this axiom is not derived from observation—there are only bodily movements to be observed but no such thing as actions—but stems instead from reflective understanding. And this understanding is indeed of a self-evident proposition. For its truth cannot be denied, since the denial would itself have to be categorized as an action. But is this not just plain trivial? And what has economics got to do with this? Of course, it had previously been recognized that economic concepts such as prices, costs, production, money, credit, etc., had something to do with the fact that there were acting people. But that all of economics could be grounded in and reconstructed based on such a trivial proposition and how, is certainly anything but clear. It is one of Mises's greatest achievements to have shown precisely this: that there are insights implied in this psychologically speaking trivial axiom of action that were not themselves psychologically self-evident as well; and that it is these insights which provide the foundation for the theorems of economics as true a priori synthetic propositions.

It is certainly not psychologically evident that with every action an actor pursues a goal; and that whatever the goal may be, the fact that it was pursued by an actor reveals that he must have placed a relatively higher value on it than on any

---

[51]On the following see in particular Mises, *Human Action*, chapter 4; Murray N. Rothbard, *Man, Economy, and State* (Los Angeles: Nash, 1962), chapter 1.

other goal of action that he could think of at the start of his action. It is not evident that in order to achieve his most highly valued goal an actor must interfere or decide not to interfere—which, of course, is also an intentional interference—at an earlier point in time in order to produce a later result; nor is it obvious that such interferences invariably imply the employment of some scarce means—at least those of the actor's body, its standing room, and the time absorbed by the action. It is not self-evident that these means, then, must also have value for an actor—a value derived from that of the goal—because the actor must regard their employment as necessary in order to effectively achieve the goal; and that actions can only be performed sequentially, always involving a choice, i.e., taking up that one course of action which at some given time promises the most highly valued results to the actor and excluding at the same time the pursual of other, less highly valued goals. It is not automatically clear that as a consequence of having to choose and give preference to one goal over another—of not being able to realize all goals simultaneously—each and every action implies the incurrence of costs, i.e., forsaking the value attached to the most highly ranking alternative goal that cannot be realized or whose realization must be deferred, because the means necessary to attain it are bound up in the production of another, even more highly valued goal. And lastly, it is not evident that at its starting point every goal of action must be considered worth more to the actor than its cost and capable of yielding a profit, i.e., a result whose value is ranked higher than that of the foregone opportunity, and yet that every action is also invariably threatened by the possibility of a loss if an actor finds, in retrospect, that contrary to his expectations the actually achieved result in fact has a lower value than the relinquished alternative would have had.

All of these categories which we know to be the very heart of economics—values, ends, means, choice, preference, cost, profit and loss—are implied in the axiom of action. Like the axiom itself, they are not derived from observation. Rather, that one is able to interpret observations in terms of such categories requires that one already knows what it means to act. No one who is not an actor could ever understand them, as they are not "given," ready to be observed, but observational experience is cast in these terms as it is construed by an actor. And while they and their interrelations were not obviously implied in the action axiom, once it has been made explicit that they are implied, and how, one no longer has any difficulty recognizing them as being a priori true in the same sense as the axiom itself is. For any attempt to disprove the validity of what Mises has reconstructed as implied in the very concept of action would have to be aimed at a goal, requiring means, excluding other courses of action, incurring costs, subjecting the actor to the possibility of achieving or not achieving the desired goal and so leading to a profit or a loss. Thus, it is manifestly impossible to ever dispute or falsify the validity of Mises's insights. In fact, a situation in which the categories of action would cease to have a real existence could itself never be observed or spoken of, since to make an observation and to speak are themselves actions.

All true economic propositions, and this is what praxeology is all about and what Mises's great insight consists of, can be deduced by means of formal logic from this incontestably true material knowledge regarding the meaning of action and its categories. More precisely, all true economic theorems consist of (a) an understanding of the meaning of action, (b) a situation or situational change—assumed to be given or identified as being given—and described in terms of action-categories, and (c) a logical deduction of the consequences—again in terms of such categories—which are to result for an actor from this situation or situational change. The law of marginal utility, for instance,[52] follows from our indisputable knowledge of the fact that every actor always prefers what satisfies him more over what satisfies him less, plus the assumption that he is faced with an increase in the supply of a good (a scarce mean) whose units he regards as of equal serviceability, by one additional unit. From this it follows with logical necessity that this additional unit can then only be employed as a means for the removal of an uneasiness that is deemed less urgent than the least valuable goal previously satisfied by a unit of such a good. Provided there is no flaw in the process of deduction, the conclusions which economic theorizing yields, no different in the case of any other economic proposition from the case of the law of marginal utility, must be valid a priori. These propositions' validity ultimately goes back to nothing but the indisputable axiom of action. To think, as empiricism does, that these propositions require continual empirical testing for their validation is absurd, and a sign of outright intellectual confusion. And it is no less absurd and confused to believe, as historicism does, that economics has nothing to say about constant and invariable relations but merely deals with historically accidental events. To say so meaningfully is to prove such a statement wrong, as saying anything meaningful at all already presupposes acting and a knowledge of the meaning of the categories of action.

III

This will suffice here as an explanation of Mises's answer regarding the quest for the foundations of economics. I shall

---

[52]On the law of marginal utility see Mises, *Human Action*, pp. 119–27 and Rothbard, *Man, Economy, and State*, pp. 268–71.

now turn to my second goal: the explanation of why and how praxeology also provides the foundation for epistemology. Mises had been aware of this and he was convinced of the great importance of this insight for rationalist philosophy. Yet Mises did not treat the matter in a systematic fashion. There are no more than a few brief remarks concerning this problem, interspersed throughout his massive body of writing.[53] Thus, in the following I must try to break new ground.

I shall begin my explanation by introducing a second a priori axiom and clarifying its relation to the axiom of action. Such an understanding is the key to solving our problem. The second axiom is the so-called "a priori of argumentation," which states that humans are capable of argumentation and hence know the meaning of truth and validity.[54] As in the case of the action axiom, this knowledge is not derived from observation: there is only verbal behavior to be observed and prior reflective cognition is required in order to interpret such behavior as meaningful arguments. And the validity of the axiom, like that of the action axiom, is indisputable. It is impossible to deny that one can argue, as the very denial would itself be an argument. In fact, one

[53]Mises writes: "Knowledge is a tool of action. Its function is to advise man how to proceed in his endeavor to remove uneasiness. . . . The category of action is the fundamental category of human knowledge. It implies all the categories of logic and the category of regularity and causality. It implies the category of time and that of value. . . . In acting, the mind of the individual sees itself as different from its environment, the external world, and tries to study this environment in order to influence the course of events happening in it" (*The Ultimate Foundation of Economic Science*, pp. 35–36). Or: "Both, apriori thinking and reasoning on the one hand and human action on the other, are manifestations of the mind. . . . Reason and action are congeneric and homogeneous, two aspects of the same phenomenon" (ibid., p.42). Yet he leaves the matter more or less at this and concludes that "it is not the scope of praxeology to investigate the relation of thinking and action" (*Human Action*, p. 25).

[54]On the a priori of argumentation see also K. O. Apel, *Transformation der Philosophie*, vol. 2.

could not even silently say to oneself "I cannot argue" without thereby contradicting oneself. One cannot argue that one cannot argue. Nor can one dispute knowing what it means to make a truth or validity claim without implicitly claiming the negation of this proposition to be true.

It is not difficult to detect that both a priori axioms—of action and argumentation—are intimately related. On the one hand, actions are more fundamental than argumentations with whose existence the idea of validity emerges, as argumentation is only a subclass of action. On the other hand, to recognize what has just been recognized regarding action and argumentation and their relation to each other requires argumentation, and so, in this sense, argumentation must be considered more fundamental than action: without argumentation nothing could be said to be known about action. But then, as it is in argumentation that the insight is revealed that—while it might not be known to be so prior to any argumentation—in fact the possibility of argumentation presupposes action in that validity claims can only be explicitly discussed in the course of an argumentation if the individuals doing so already know what it means to act and to have knowledge implied in action—both the meaning of action in general and argumentation in particular must be thought of as logically necessary interwoven strands of a priori knowledge.

What this insight into the interrelation between the a priori of action and the a priori of argumentation suggests is the following: Traditionally, the task of epistemology has been conceived of as that of formulating what can be known to be true a priori and also what can be known a priori not to be the subject of a priori knowledge. Recognizing, as we have just done, that knowledge claims are raised and decided upon in the course of argumentation and that this is undeniably so, one can now reconstruct the task of epistemology more precisely as that of formulating those propositions which are argumentatively indisputable in that their truth is already implied in the very fact of making one's argument and so cannot be denied argumentatively; and to delineate the range of such a priori knowledge from the realm of propositions whose validity cannot be established in this way but require additional, contingent information for their validation, or that cannot be validated at all and so are mere metaphysical statements in the pejorative sense of the term metaphysical.

Yet what is implied in the very fact of arguing? It is to this question that our insight into the inextricable interconnection between the a priori of argumentation and that of action provides an answer: On a very general level, it cannot be denied argumentatively that argumentation presupposes action and that arguments, and the knowledge embodied in them, are those of actors. And more specifically, it cannot then be denied that knowledge itself is a category of action; that the structure of knowledge must be constrained by the peculiar function which knowledge fulfills within the framework of action categories; and that the existence of such structural constraints can never be disproved by any knowledge whatsoever.

It is in this sense that the insights contained in praxeology must be regarded as providing the foundations of epistemology. Knowledge is a category quite distinct from those that I have explained earlier—from ends and means. The ends which we strive to attain through our actions, and the means which we employ in order to do so, are both scarce values. The values attached to our goals are subject to consumption and are exterminated and destroyed in consumption and thus must forever be produced anew. And the means employed must be economized, too. Not so, however, with respect to knowledge—regardless of whether one considers it a means or an end in itself. Of course, the acquisition of knowledge requires scarce means—at least one's body and time. Yet once knowledge is acquired, it is no longer scarce. It can neither be consumed, nor are the services that it can render as a means subject to depletion. Once there, it is an inexhaustible resource and incorporates an everlasting value provided that it is not simply forgotten.[55] Yet knowledge is not a free good in the same sense that air, under normal circumstances, is a free good. Instead, it is a category of action. It is not only a mental ingredient of each and every action, quite unlike air, but more importantly, knowledge, and not air, is subject to validation, which is to say that it must prove to fulfill a positive function for an actor within the invariant constraints of the categorical framework of actions. It is the task of epistemology to clarify what these constraints are and what one can thus know about the structure of knowledge as such.

While such recognition of the praxeological constraints on the structure of knowledge might not immediately strike one as in itself of great significance, it does have some highly important implications. For one thing, in light of this insight one recurring difficulty of rationalist philosophy finds its answer. It has been a common quarrel with rationalism in the Leibniz–Kant tradition that it seemed to imply some sort of idealism. Realizing that a priori true propositions could not possibly be derived from observations, rationalism answered the question how a priori knowledge could then be possible by adopting the model of an active mind, as opposed

---

[55]On this fundamental difference between economic, i.e., scarce means and knowledge, see also Mises, *Human Action*, pp. 128, 661.

to the empiricist model of a passive, mirror-like mind in the tradition of Locke and Hume. According to rationalist philosophy, a priori true propositions had their foundation in the operation of principles of thinking which one could not possibly conceive of as operating otherwise; they were grounded in categories of an active mind. Now, as empiricists were only too eager to point out, the obvious critique of such a position is, that if this were indeed the case, it could not be explained why such mental categories should fit reality. Rather, one would be forced to accept the absurd idealistic assumption that reality would have to be conceived of as a creation of the mind, in order to claim that a priori knowledge could incorporate any information about the structure of reality. And clearly, such an assertion seemed to be justified when faced with programmatic statements of rationalist philosophers such as the following by Kant: "So far it has been assumed that our knowledge had to conform to reality," instead it should be assumed "that observational reality should conform to our mind."[56]

Recognizing knowledge as being structurally constrained by its role in the framework of action categories provides the solution to such a complaint. For as soon as this is realized, all idealistic suggestions of rationalist philosophy disappear, and an epistemology claiming that a priori true propositions exist becomes a realistic epistemology instead. Understood as constrained by action categories, the seemingly unbridgeable gulf between the mental on the one hand and the real, outside physical world on the other is bridged. So constrained, a priori knowledge must

---

[56]Immanuel Kant, *Kritik der reinen Vernunft*, p. 25. Whether or not such an interpretation of Kant's epistemology is indeed correct is, of course, a very different matter. Clarifying this problem is, however, of no concern here. For an activist or constructivist interpretation of Kantian philosophy see F. Kambartel, *Erfahrung und Struktur*, chapter 3; also Hoppe, *Handeln und Erkennen* (Bern: Lang, 1976).

be as much a mental thing as a reflection of the structure of reality, since it is only through actions that the mind comes into contact with reality, so to speak. Acting is a cognitively guided adjustment of a physical body in physical reality. And thus, there can be no doubt that a priori knowledge, conceived of as an insight into the structural constraints imposed on knowledge qua knowledge of actors, must indeed correspond to the nature of things. The realistic character of such knowledge would manifest itself not only in the fact that one could not *think* it to be otherwise, but in the fact that one could not *undo* its truth.

Yet there are more specific implications involved in recognizing the praxeological foundations of epistemology—apart from the general one that in substituting the model of the mind of an actor acting by means of a physical body for the traditional rationalist model of an active mind a priori knowledge immediately becomes realistic knowledge (so realistic indeed that it can be understood as being literally not undoable). More specifically, in light of this insight decisive support is given to those deplorably few rationalist philosophers who—against the empiricist Zeitgeist—stubbornly maintain on various philosophical fronts that a priori true propositions about the real world are possible.[57] Moreover, in

---

[57]In addition to the works mentioned in note 46 see Brand Blanshard, *The Nature of Thought* (London: Allen and Unwin, 1921); M. Cohen, *Reason and Nature* (New York: Harcourt, Brace, 1931); idem, *Preface to Logic* (New York: Holt, 1944); A. Pap, *Semantics and Necessary Truth* (New Haven: Yale University Press, 1958); S. Kripke, "Naming and Necessity," in D. Davidson and G. Harman, eds., *Semantics of Natural Language* (New York: Reidel, 1972); H. Dingler, *Die Ergreifung des Wirklichen* (Frankfurt/M.: Suhrkamp, 1969); idem, *Aufbau der exakten Fundamentalwissenschaft* (Munich: Eidos, 1964); W. Kamlah and P. Lorenzen, *Logische Propädeutik Mannheim:* (Mannheim: Bibliographisches Institut, 1968); P. Lorenzen, *Methodisches Denken* (Frankfurt/M.: Suhrkamp, 1968); idem, *Normative Logic and Ethics* (Mannheim: Bibliographisches Institut, 1969); K. O. Apel, *Transformation der Philosophie*.

---

light of the recognition of praxeological constraints on the structure of knowledge these various rationalist endeavors become systematically integrated into one, unified body of rationalist philosophy.

In explicitly understanding knowledge as displayed in argumentation as a peculiar category of action, it becomes clear immediately why the perennial rationalist claim that the laws of logic—beginning here with the most fundamental ones, i.e., of propositional logic and of Junctors ("and," "or," "if-then," "not") and Quantors ("there is," "all," "some")—are a priori true propositions about reality and not mere verbal stipulations regarding the transformation rules of arbitrarily chosen signs, as empiricist-formalists would have it, is indeed correct. They are as much laws of thinking as of reality, because they are laws that have their ultimate foundation in action and could not be undone by any actor. In each and every action, an actor identifies some specific situation and categorizes it one way rather than another in order to be able to make a choice. It is this which ultimately explains the structure of even the most elementary propositions (like "Socrates is a man") consisting of a proper name or some identifying expression for the naming or identifying of something, and a predicate to assert or deny some specific property of the named or identified object; and which explains the cornerstones of logic: the laws of identity and contradiction. And it is this universal feature of action and choosing which also explains our understanding of the categories "there is," "all" and, by implication, "some," as well as "and," "or," "if-then" and "not."[58] One can *say*,

---

[58]On rationalist interpretations of logic see Blanshard, *Reason and Analysis*, chapters 6, 10; P. Lorenzen, *Einführung in die operative Logik und Mathematik* (Frankfurt/M.: Akademische Verlagsgesellschaft, 1970); K. Lorenz, *Elemente der Sprachkritik* (Frankfurt/M.: Suhrkamp, 1970); idem, "Die dialogische Rechtfertigung der effektiven Logik," in: F. Kambartel and J. Mittelstrass, eds., *Zum normativen Fundament der Wissenschaft* (Frankfurt/M.: Athenäum, 1973).

of course, that something can be "a" and "non-a" at the same time, or that "and" means this rather than something else. But one cannot *undo* the law of contradiction; and one cannot undo the real definition of "and." For simply by virtue of acting with a physical body in physical space we invariably affirm the law of contradiction and invariably display our true constructive knowledge of the meaning of "and" and "or."

Similarly, the ultimate reason for arithmetic's being an a priori and yet empirical discipline, as rationalists have

---

On the propositional character of language and experience, in particular, see W. Kamlah and P. Lorenzen, *Logische Propädeutik,* chapter 1; P. Lorenzen, *Normative Logic and Ethics,* chapter 1. Lorenzen writes: "I call a usage a convention if I know of another usage which I could accept instead. . . . However, I do not know of another behavior which could replace the use of elementary sentences. If I did not accept proper names and predicators, I would not know how to speak at all. . . . Each proper name is a convention . . . but to use proper names at all is not a convention: it is a unique pattern of linguistic behavior. Therefore, I am going to call it 'logical'. The same is true with predicators. Each predicator is a convention. This is shown by the existence of more than one natural language. But all languages use predicators" (ibid., p. 16). See also J. Mittelstrass, "Die Wiederkehr des Gleichen," *Ratio* (1966).

On the law of identity and contradiction, in particular, see B. Blanshard, *Reason and Analysis*, pp. 276ff, 423ff.

On a critical evaluation of 3- or more-valued logics as either meaningless symbolic formalisms or as logically presupposing an understanding of the traditional two-valued logic see W. Stegmüller, *Hauptströmungen der Gegenwartsphilosophie* vol. 2 (Stuttgart: Kröner, 1975), pp. 182–91; B. Blanshard, *Reason and Analysis*, pp. 269–75. Regarding, for instance, the many-valued or open-textured logic, proposed by F. Waismann, Blanshard notes: "We can only agree with Dr. Waismann—and with Hegel—that the black-and-white distinctions of formal logic are quite inadequate to living thought. But why should one say, as Dr. Waismann does, that in adopting a more differentiated logic one is adopting an alternative system which is incompatible with black-and-white logic? What he has actually done is to recognize a number of gradations *within* the older meaning of the word 'not'. We do not doubt that such gradations are there, and indeed as many more as he cares to distinguish. But a refinement of the older logic is not an abandonment of it. It is still true that the colour I saw yesterday was either a determinate shade of yellow or not, even though the 'not' may cover a multitude of approximations, and even though I shall never know which was the shade I saw" (ibid., pp. 273–74).

---

always understood it, now also becomes discernible. The prevailing empiricist-formalist orthodoxy conceives of arithmetic as the manipulation of arbitrarily defined signs according to arbitrarily stipulated transformation rules, and thus as entirely void of any empirical meaning. For this view, which evidently makes arithmetic nothing but play, however skillful it might be, the successful applicability of arithmetic in physics is an intellectual embarrassment. Indeed, empiricist-formalists would have to explain away this fact as simply being a miraculous event. That it is no miracle, however, becomes apparent once the praxeological or—to use here the terminology of the most notable rationalist philosopher-mathematician Paul Lorenzen and his school—the operative or constructivist character of arithmetic is understood. Arithmetic and its character as an a priori–synthetic intellectual discipline is rooted in our understanding of repetition, the repetition of action. More precisely, it rests on our understanding the meaning of "do this—and do this again, starting from the present result." And arithmetic then deals with real things: with constructed or constructively identified units of something. It demonstrates what relations are to hold between such units because of the fact that they are constructed according to the rule of repetition. As Paul Lorenzen has demonstrated in detail, not all of what presently poses as mathematics can be constructively founded—and those parts, then, should of course be recognized for what they are: epistemologically worthless symbolic games. But all of the mathematical tools that are actually employed in physics, i.e., the tools of classical analysis, can be constructively derived. They are not empirically void symbolisms, but true propositions about reality. They apply to everything insofar as it consists of one or more distinct units, and insofar as these units are constructed or identified as units by a procedure of "do it again, construct or identify another unit by repeating the previous operation."[59] Again, one can *say*, of course, that 2 plus 2 is sometimes 4 but sometimes 2 or 5 units, and in observational reality, for lions plus lambs or for rabbits, this may even be true,[60] but in the reality of action, in identifying or constructing those units in repetitive operations, the truth that 2 plus 2 is never anything but 4 could not possibly be undone.

Further, the old rationalist claims that geometry, that is, Euclidean geometry is a priori and yet incorporates empirical knowledge about space becomes supported, too, in view of our insight into the praxeological constraints on knowledge. Since the discovery of non-Euclidean geometries and

---

[59]On a rationalist interpretation of arithmetic see Blanshard, *Reason and Analysis,* pp. 427–31; on the constructivist foundation of arithmetic, in particular, see Lorenzen, *Einführung in die operative Logik und Mathematik*; idem, *Methodisches Denken,* chapters 6, 7; idem, *Normative Logic and Ethics,* chapter 4; on the constructivist foundation of classical analysis see P. Lorenzen, *Differential und Integral: Eine konstruktive Einführung in die klassische Analysis* (Frankfurt/M.: Akademische Verlagsgesellschaft, 1965); for a brilliant general critique of mathematical formalism see Kambartel, *Erfahrung und Struktur,* chapter 6, esp. pp. 236–42; on the irrelevance of the famous Gödel-theorem for a constructively founded arithmetic see P. Lorenzen, *Metamathematik* (Mannheim: Bibliographisches Institut, 1962); also Ch. Thiel, "Das Begründungsproblem der Mathematik und die Philosophie," in F. Kambartel and J. Mittelstrass, eds., *Zum normativen Fundament der Wissenschaft,* esp. pp. 99–101. K. Gödel's proof—which, as a proof, incidentally supports rather than undermines the rationalist claim of the possibility of *a priori* knowledge—only demonstrates that the early formalist Hilbert program cannot be successfully carried through, because in order to demonstrate the consistency of certain axiomatic theories one must have a metatheory with even stronger means than those formalized in the object-theory itself. Interestingly enough, the difficulties of the formalist program had led the old Hilbert already several years before Gödel's proof of 1931 to recognize the necessity of reintroducing a substantive interpretation of mathematics à la Kant, which would give its axioms a foundation and justification that was entirely independent of any formal consistency proofs. See Kambartel, *Erfahrung und Struktur,* pp. 185–87.

[60]Examples of this kind are used by Karl Popper in order to "refute" the rationalist idea of rules of arithmetic being laws of reality. See Karl Popper, *Conjectures and Refutations* (London: Routledge and Kegan Paul, 1969), p. 211.

---

in particular since Einstein's relativistic theory of gravitation, the prevailing position regarding geometry is once again empiricist and formalist. It conceives of geometry as either being part of empirical, aposteriori physics, or as being empirically meaningless formalisms. Yet that geometry is either mere play, or forever subject to empirical testing seems to be irreconcilable with the fact that Euclidean geometry is the foundation of engineering and construction, and that nobody there ever thinks of such propositions as only hypothetically true.[61] Recognizing knowledge as praxeologically constrained explains why the empiricist-formalist view is incorrect and why the empirical success of Euclidean geometry is no mere accident. Spatial knowledge is also included in the meaning of action. Action is the employment of a physical body in space. Without acting there could be no knowledge of spatial relations, and no measurement. Measuring is relating something to a standard. Without standards, there is no measurement; and there is no measurement, then, which could ever falsify the standard. Evidently, the ultimate standard must be provided by the norms underlying the construction of bodily movements in space and the construction of measurement instruments by means of one's body and in accordance with the principles of spatial constructions embodied in it. Euclidean geometry, as again Paul Lorenzen in particular has explained, is no more and no less than the reconstruction of the ideal norms underlying our construction of such homogeneous basic forms as points, lines, planes and distances, which are in a more or less perfect but always perfectible way incorporated or realized in even our most primitive instruments of spatial measurements such as a measuring rod. Naturally,

---

[61]See on this also Mises, *The Ultimate Foundation of Economic Science,* pp. 12–14.

these norms and normative implications cannot be falsified by the result of any empirical measurement. On the contrary, their cognitive validity is substantiated by the fact that it is they which make physical measurements in space possible. Any actual measurement must already presuppose the validity of the norms leading to the construction of one's measurement standards. It is in this sense that geometry is an a priori science; and that it must simultaneously be regarded as an empirically meaningful discipline, because it is not only the very precondition for any empirical spatial description, it is also the precondition for any active orientation in space.[62]

In view of the recognition of the praxeological character of knowledge, these insights regarding the nature of logic, arithmetic and geometry become integrated and embedded into a system of epistemological dualism.[63] The ultimate

---

[62]On the aprioristic character of Euclidean geometry see Lorenzen, *Methodisches Denken*, chapters 8 and 9; idem, *Normative Logic and Ethics*, chapter 5; H. Dingler, *Die Grundlagen der Geometrie* (Stuttgart: Enke, 1933); on Euclidean geometry as a necessary presupposition of objective, i.e., intersubjectively communicable, measurements and in particular of any empirical verification of non-Euclidean geometries (after all, the lenses of the telescopes which one uses to confirm Einstein's theory regarding the non-Euclidean structure of physical space must themselves be constructed according to Euclidean principles) see Kambartel, *Erfahrung und Struktur*, pp. 132–33; P. Janich, *Die Protophysik der Zeit* (Mannheim: Bibliographisches Institut, 1969), pp. 45–50; idem, "Eindeutigkeit, Konsistenz und methodische Ordnung," in F. Kambartel and J. Mittelstrass, eds., *Zum normativen Fundament der Wissenschaft*.

Following the lead of Hugo Dingler, Paul Lorenzen and other members of the so-called Erlangen school have worked out a system of protophysics, which contains all aprioristic presuppositions of empirical physics, including, apart from geometry, also chronometry and hylometry (i.e., classical mechanics without gravitation, or "rational" mechanics). "Geometry, chronometry and hylometry are a-priori theories which make empirical measurements of space, time and materia 'possible'. They have to be established before physics in the modern sense of an empirical science, with hypothetical fields of forces, can begin. Therefore, I should like to call these disciplines by a common name: protophysics." Lorenzen, *Normative Logic and Ethics*, p. 60.

[63]On the fundamental nature of epistemological dualism see also Mises, *Theory and History*, pp. 1–2.

---

justification for this dualist position, i.e., the claim that there are two realms of intellectual inquiry that can be understood a priori as requiring categorically distinct methods of treatment and analysis, also lies in the praxeological nature of knowledge. It explains why we must differentiate between a realm of objects which is categorized causally and a realm that is categorized teleologically instead.

I have already briefly indicated during my discussion of praxeology that *causality* is a category of action. The idea of causality that there are constant, time-invariantly operating causes which allow one to project past observations regarding the relation of events into the future is something (as empiricism since Hume has noticed) which has no observational basis whatsoever. One cannot observe the connecting link between observations. Even if one could, such an observation would not prove it to be a time-invariant connection. Instead, the principle of causality must be understood as implied in our understanding of action as an interference with the observational world, made with the intent of diverting the "natural" course of events in order to produce a different, prefered state of affairs, i.e., of making things happen that otherwise would not happen, and thus presupposes the notion of events which are related to each other through time-invariantly operating causes. An actor might err with respect to his particular assumptions about which earlier interference produced which later result. But successful or not, any action, changed or unchanged in light of its previous success or failure, presupposes that there are constantly connected events *as such*, even if no particular cause for any particular event can ever be preknown to any actor. Without such an assumption it would be impossible to ever categorize two or more observational experiences as falsifying or confirming each other rather than interpreting them as logically incommensurable events. Only because the existence of time-invariantly operating causes as such is already assumed can one ever encounter particular instances of confirming or disconfirming observational evidence, or can there ever be an actor who can learn anything from past experience by classifying his actions as successful and confirming some previous knowledge, or unsuccessful and disconfirming it. It is simply by virtue of acting and distinguishing between successes and failures that the a priori validity of the principle of causality is established; even if one tried, one could not successfully refute its validity.[64]

In so understanding causality as a necessary presupposition of action, it is also immediately implied that its range of applicability must then be delineated a priori from that of the category of teleology. Indeed, both categories are strictly exclusive and complementary. Action presupposes a causally structured observational reality, but the reality of action which we can understand as requiring such structure, is not itself causally structured. Instead, it is a reality that must be categorized teleologically, as purpose-directed, meaningful behavior. In fact, one can neither deny nor undo

---

[64]On the aprioristic character of the category of causality see Mises, *Human Action*, chapter 1; Hoppe, *Kritik der kausalwissenschaftlichen Sozialforschung;* idem, "Is Research Based on Causal Scientic Principles Possible in the Social Sciences?"; on the causality principle as a necessary presupposition in particular also of the indeterminacy principle of quantum physics and the fundamental misconception involved in interpreting the Heisenberg-principle as invalidating the causality principle see Kambartel, *Erfahrung und Struktur,* pp. 138–40; also Hoppe, "In Defense of Extreme Rationalism," footnote 36. In fact, it is precisely the indisputable praxeological fact that separate measurement acts can only be performed sequentially which explains the very possibility of irreducibly probabilistic–rather than deterministic–predictions as they are characteristic of quantum physics; and yet, in order to perform any experiments in the field of quantum mechanics, and in particular to repeat two or more experiments and state this to be the case, the validity of the causality principle must evidently already be presupposed.

the view that there are two categorically different realms of phenomena, since such attempts would have to presuppose causally related events qua actions that take place within observational reality, as well as the existence of intentionally rather than causally related phenomena in order to interpret such observational events as meaning to deny something. Neither a causal, nor a teleological monism could be justified without running into an open contradiction: physically stating either position, and claiming to say something meaningful in so doing, the case is in fact made for an indisputable complementarity of both, a realm of causal *and* teleological phenomena.[65]

Everything which is not an action must necessarily be categorized causally. There is nothing to be known a priori about this range of phenomena except that it is structured causally—and that it is structured according to the categories of propositional logic, arithmetic and geometry.[66] Everything else there is to know about this range of phenomena must be derived from contingent observations and thus represents aposteriori knowledge. In particular, all knowledge about two or more specific observational events being causally related or not is aposteriori knowledge. Obviously, the range of phenomena described in this way coincides (more or less) with what is usually considered to be the field of the empirical natural sciences.

[65]On the necessary complementarity of the categories of causality and teleology see Mises, *Human Action*, p. 25; idem, *The Ultimate Foundation of Economic Science,* pp. 6–8; Hoppe, *Kritik der kausalwissenschaftlichen Sozialforschung*; idem, "Is Research Based on Causal Scientific Principles Possible in the Social Sciences?"; also G. v. Wright, *Norm and Action* (London: Routledge and Kegan Paul, 1963); idem, *Explanation and Understanding* (Ithaca, N.Y.: Cornell University Press, 1971); K. O. Apel, *Die Erklären: Verstehen Kontroverse in transzendental-pragmatischer Sicht* (Frankfurt/M.: Suhrkamp, 1979).

[66]More precisely still: it is structured according to the categories of logic, arithmetic, and protophysics (including geometry). See note 62 above.

In contrast, everything that is an action must be categorized teleologically. This realm of phenomena is constrained
by the laws of logic and arithmetic, too. But it is not
constrained by the laws of geometry as incorporated in our
instruments of measuring spatially extending objects, because actions do not exist apart from subjective interpretations of observable things; and so they must be identified
by reflective understanding rather than spatial measurements. Nor are actions causally connected events, but events
that are connected meaningfully within a categorical framework of means and ends.

One can *not* know a priori what the *specific* values,
choices and costs of some actor are or will be. This would
fall entirely into the province of empirical, aposteriori
knowledge. In fact, which particular action an actor is going
to undertake would depend on his knowledge regarding the
observational reality and/or the reality of other actors' actions. And it would be manifestly impossible to conceive of
such states of knowledge as predictable on the basis of
time-invariantly operating causes. A knowing actor cannot
predict his future knowledge before he has actually acquired
it, and he demonstrates, simply by virtue of distinguishing
between successful and unsuccessful predictions, that he
must conceive of himself as capable of learning from unknown experiences in as yet unknown ways. Thus, knowledge regarding the particular course of actions is only
aposteriori. And since such knowledge would have to in-
clude the actor's own knowledge—as a necessary ingredient
of every action whose every change can have an influence
on a particular action being chosen—teleological knowledge
must also necessarily be reconstructive, or historical knowledge. It would only provide ex-post explanations which
would have no systematic bearing on the prediction of

future actions, because, in principle, future states of knowledge could never be predicted on the basis of constantly operating empirical causes. Obviously, such a delineation of a branch of aposteriori and reconstructive science of action fits the usual description of such disciplines as history and sociology.[67]

What *is* known to be true a priori regarding the field of action, and what would then have to constrain any historical or sociological explanation is this: For one thing, any such explanation, which essentially would have to reconstruct an actor's knowledge, would invariably have to be a reconstruction in terms of knowledge of ends and means, of choices and costs, of profits and losses and so on. And secondly, since these are evidently the categories of praxeology as conceived of by Mises, any such explanation must also be constrained by the laws of praxeology. And since these laws are, as I have already explained, a priori laws, they must also operate as logical constraints on any future course of action. They are valid independent of any specific state of knowledge that an actor might have acquired, simply by virtue of the fact that whatever this state might be, it must be described in terms of action categories. And as referring to actions as such, the laws of praxeology must then be coextensive with all the predictive knowledge there can be in the field of the science of action. In fact, ignoring for the moment that the status of geometry as an a priori science was ultimately grounded in our understanding of action and in so far praxeology would have to be regarded as the more fundamental cognitive discipline, the peculiar role of

---

[67]On the logic of history and sociology as reconstructive disciplines see in addition to the works of Mises mentioned at the outset of this chapter Hoppe, *Kritik der kausalwissenschaftlichen Sozialforschung*, chapter 2.

praxeology proper within the entire system of epistemology can be understood as somewhat analogous to that of geometry. Praxeology is for the field of action what Euclidean geometry is for the field of observations (non-actions). As the geometry incorporated in our measuring instruments constrains the spatial structure of observational reality, so praxeology constrains the range of things that can possibly be experienced in the field of actions.[68]

IV

In so establishing the place of praxeology proper, I have come full circle in outlining the system of rationalist philosophy as ultimately grounded in the action axiom. It has been my goal here to reaffirm Mises's claim that economics is praxeology; that the case for praxeology is an indisputable one; and that empiricist or historicist-hermeneuticist interpretations of economics are self-contradictory doctrines. And it has been my objective to indicate that the Misesian insight into the nature of praxeology also provides the very foundation on which traditional rationalist philosophy can be successfully reconstructed, and systematically integrated.

For the rationalist philosopher this would seem to imply that he should take account of praxeology. For it is precisely the insight into the praxeological constraints on the structure of knowledge which provides the missing link in his intellectual defense against skepticism and relativism. For

---

[68]On the categorical distinctiveness of praxeological theory and history and sociology and the logical constraints that praxeology imposes on historical and sociological research as well as on social and economic predictions see Mises, *Human Action*, pp. 51–59, 117–18; Hoppe, "In Defense of Extreme Rationalism."

the economist in the tradition of Mises it means, I claim, that he should explicitly come to recognize his place within the wider tradition of western rationalism; and that he should learn to incorporate the insights provided by this tradition in order to construct an even more impressive and profound case for praxeology and Austrian economics than the one made by the great Mises himself.

Recommended Readings

Block, Walter. "On Robert Nozick's 'On Austrian Methodology'." *Inquiry* 23 (1980).

Hollis, Martin, and Edward Nell. *Rational Economic Man: A Philosophical Critique of Neo-Classical Economics*. Cambridge: Cambridge University Press, 1975.

Hoppe, Hans-Hermann. *Kritik der kausalwissenschaftlichen Sozialforschung. Unterschungen zur Grundlegung von Soziologie und Ökonomie*. Opladen: Westdeutscher Verlag, 1983.

——. "Is Research Based on Causal Scientific Principles Possible in the Social Sciences?" *Ratio* 25, no. 1 (1983).

——. "In Defense of Extreme Rationalism." *Review of Austrian Economics* 3 (1988).

——. *A Theory of Socialism and Capitalism*. Kluwer Academic Publishers, 1989.

——. "On Praxeology and the Praxeological Foundations of Epistemology and Ethics." In Llewellyn H. Rockwell, Jr., ed., *The Meaning of Ludwig von Mises*. Auburn, Ala.: Ludwig von Mises Institute, 1989.

——. *The Economics and Ethics of Private Property*. Kluwer Academic Publishers, 1993.

Kirzner, Israel M. *The Economic Point of View*. Kansas City, Kans.: Sheed and Ward, 1976.

Lavoie, Don. "From Hollis and Nell to Hollis and Mises." *Journal of Libertarian Studies*, I, no. 4 (1977).

Mises, Ludwig von. *Epistemological Problems of Economics*. New York: New York University Press, 1981.

——. *Human Action: A Treatise on Economics*. Chicago: Henry Regnery, 1966; Part 1.

—. *Theory and History*. Washington, D.C.: Ludwig von Mises Institute, [1969] 1985.

—. *The Ultimate Foundation of Economic Science*. Kansas City, Kans.: Sheed Andrews and McMeel, 1978.

Rizzo, Mario. "Praxeology and Econometrics: A Critique of Positivist Economics." In Louis M. Spadaro, ed., *New Directions in Austrian Economics*. Kansas City, Kans.: Sheed Andrews and McMeel, 1978.

Robbins, Lionel. *The Nature and Significance of Economic Science*. New York: New York University Press, 1984.

Rothbard, Murray N. "Praxeology: Reply to Mr. Schuller." *American Economic Review*, December 1951.

—. "In Defense of Extreme Apriorism." *Southern Economic Journal* 23, no. 3 (January 1957).

—. *Man, Economy, and State*. 2 Vols. Los Angeles: Nash 1970 [1962]; Chapter 1.

—. "Praxeology: The Methodology of Austrian Economics." In Edwin Dolan, ed., *The Foundations of Modern Austrian Economics*. Kansas City, Kans.: Sheed and Ward, 1976.

—. *Individualism and the Philosophy of the Social Sciences*. San Francisco: Cato Institute, 1979.

Selgin, George. "Praxeology and Understanding: An Analysis of the Controversy in Austrian Economics." *Review of Austrian Economics* 2 (1987).

Strigl, Richard von. *Die ökonomischen Kategorien und die Organisation der Wirtschaft*. Jena: Gustav Fischer, 1923.

INDEX

Albert, H., 10
Andreski, St., 54
Apel, K. O., 38, 43, 57, 65,
    70, 79
Aposteriori propositions, 17,
    79, 80
A priori of argumentation, 65–67
A priori propositions, 17, 35
A priorism, 8, 9, 10, 11,
    14–15, 24–26, 44, 60,
    69–71, 81
A priori synthetic proposi-
    tions, 19–25, 35, 59
Analytic propositions, 17, 33
Austrian school, 7–8, 27
Axiom of action, 21–25,
    61–63, 67
Ayer, Alfred J., 28

Barnes, J., 54
Blalock, H. B., 36
Blanshard, Brand, 33, 56, 70,
    71, 72, 74
Blaug, Mark, 9, 51
Böhm-Bawerk, Eugen von, 12

Cairnes, John Elliott, 10,
    11–12, 55
Carnap, R., 28
Causality, 18, 21, 29–32,
    36–38, 77–79
Chomsky, Noam, 43
Cohen, M., 70

Comparative advantage
    (Ricardian law of associa-
    tion), 14, 16

Data analysis, 31–32
Davidson, D., 70
Dingler, Hugo, 21, 35, 70, 76
Dolan, Edwin, 56
Duncan, O., 36

Empiricism, 13–14, 28–31,
    51–53.
    criticisms of, 33–38, 55–57
Epistemology, 17–21, 49–50,
    65–83

Forecasting, 31–32, 38–40,
    43–48, 79
Friedman, Milton, 31, 51

Geometry, 18, 74–76, 80,
    81–82
Godel, K., 74
Goldberger, A., 36
Gordon, David, 54

Habermas, Jürgen, 42, 43, 57
Harman, G., 70
Hempel, C. G., 28
Hermeneutics 53–54, 58
Historicism 31, 53–55
    criticisms of, 57–59
History, 31–32, 40–43
Hollis, Martin, 33, 56

ABOUT THE AUTHOR

Hans-Hermann Hoppe is an Austrian School economist and libertarian/anarcho-capitalist philosopher. He is professor of economics at the University of Nevada, Las Vegas, a distinguished fellow with the Ludwig von Mises Institute, founder and president of the Property and Freedom Society, and editor-at-large of the *Journal of Libertarian Studies*.

He was born on September 2, 1949, in Peine, Germany. He attended the Universität des Saarlandes, Saarbrücken, the Goethe-Universität, Frankfurt/M., and the University of Michigan, Ann Arbor, for studies in philosophy, sociology, history, and economics. He earned his Ph.D. (philosophy 1974) and his "Habilitation" (sociology and economics, 1981), both from the Goethe-Universität, Frankfurt/M.

Professor Hoppe is the author of *Handeln und Erkennen* (1976); *Kritik der kausalwissenschaftlichen Sozialforschung* (1983); *Eigentum, Anarchie und Staat* (1987); *Theory of Socialism and Capitalism* (1988); *The Economics and Ethics of Private Property* (1993; 2nd ed. 2006); *Democracy–The God That Failed* (2001); *The Myth of National Defense* (2003); and numerous articles on philosophy, economics, and the social sciences.